Give YourSelf Permission Anthology

44 Inspirational and Insightful True Stories of
Risk-Taking, Life Changes and Successful Outcomes

Priya Rana Kapoor

&

Nanette Stein

Permission Media, Inc.

Give YourSelf Permission® books may be ordered through booksellers or by contacting:
Permission Media, Inc.
4180 Via Real
Carpinteria, CA 93013
www.GYSPermission.com
1 (805) 895-9338

Because of the dynamic nature of the Internet, any web addresses or links contained in this book may have changed since publication and may no longer be valid. The views expressed in this work are solely those of the authors and do not necessarily reflect the views of the publisher, and the publisher hereby disclaims any responsibility for them.

The author of each story in this book does not dispense medical advice or prescribe the use of any technique as a form of treatment for physical, emotional, or medical problems without the advice of a physician, either directly or indirectly. The intent of the authors is only to offer information of a general nature to help you in your quest for emotional and spiritual wellbeing.

In the event you use any of the information in this book for yourself, which is your constitutional right, the authors and the publisher assume no responsibility for your actions.

Image of Terri Gurrola AP Photo/The Journal & Constitution, Louie Favorite © Associated Press.

First edition 2016
10 9 8 7 6 5 4 3 2 1

ISBN: 978-0-9971-3400-1 (sc)
ISBN: 978-0-9971-3401-8 (e)

Library of Congress Control Number: 2015959971

Permission Media, Inc. rev. date: 9/26/2016

In Memory of
Joseph P. Allen & Melissa Contreras McGavin, Ph.D.

and

For all those seeking permission
and finding it within themselves.

Contents

Preface

We go to work, we pay our mortgages, feed and educate our children and try our best to lead happy and fulfilling lives.

But here's a question for you: Are we giving ourselves permission to live our OWN life and live it to the fullest? Our humble contribution comes from a thought that, if enough of us can share our stories, we do have a chance to enhance other people's lives and in turn these stories might inspire you to do something different.

We put out an open invitation to collate stories and essays in order to share, teach, learn and inspire. Our contributors are not always experts and might not give lectures — they are people like you and me who are able to look at people and things that have helped them along life's highway, and have been able to put down in words an opportunity for us to connect.

The next time you are in a queue in a supermarket, cinema or at the post office, be aware of the fact that the person in front or behind you probably has a remarkable story to tell.

As Anthony W. Richardson put it, *"The behavior of others provides a rich source of information that individuals can use to improve their behavior without direct experience."*

Innovation has changed the publishing industry although we still love books as more has *not* changed than has changed. This anthology is all about people and, as Peter Diamandis has recently observed, *"Humans haven't had a software update in 200,000 years."* This is why we prefer to publish this in book format rather than give you bite sized tweets and quotes.

We all have dreams, ambitions and aspirations and that has not changed. Our goal here is to be mindful of you the reader and to reach, move and affect you with strong messages and inspiring content.

Our heartfelt thanks go out to all of the contributors.

James Charles Darnborough,
Publisher, Permission Media, Inc.

Introduction

Everybody has a story, people just want to be heard and many want to know they are not alone. This is why we have compiled this book of 44 inspirational and insightful stories. I asked each author to be open and honest in their story telling. They have exposed their vulnerabilities and shared their challenges, but at the same time we, the readers, have the privilege of sharing their success. All the while we learn from their humbleness and spirit.

These are strong and powerful stories of how and why each individual gave themselves permission to do something out of the ordinary, something that was not expected of them by their family or society, or that they did not even expect of themselves.

In a way, this phrase "Give YourSelf Permission" is a life hack. It seems so simple but can be quite difficult to do. We worry so much about what other people think of us. We fear the possibility of change or even making a mistake, and I understand that. But as you read these stories I'm going to ask you to step into the author's shoes, live their lives and understand their decisions. You may not agree with them, but you may come to have empathy for what they went through. Celebrate their achievements with the idea that you, too, can make the changes necessary to live your life, the way you want to — and have wonderful relationships as you do.

So, before we go any further, let me ask you, if I were to call you up and ask you to write a story for the next anthology collection, what would you write about? Where have you given yourself permission to do something that you never thought previously possible? What have you done to change the course of your life and possibly the life of those around you? Where have you empowered yourself to move beyond your comfort zone? And, what exactly did you have to decide to do? Because that is what giving yourself permission is all about, it a decision — a choice you need to make. So often we wait for others to give us permission, but at our core we need to give it to ourselves. Even if you think you have not done something out of the ordinary, I know you have. As you read the following stories think about where you have shone, too.

When you give yourself permission to do something in a different way, and step into that arena of your life, then you are half-way there. It's a big step, but arguably one of the hardest. So, what are you going to give yourself permission to do in your life? Say it out loud and hold it in your heart. Be very clear on what you want to give yourself permission to do — it's known as having clear intention.

In 2014, I published my own book, *Give YourSelf Permission to Live Your Life* (Balboa Press). The first few chapters outline my own life story, how I came to give myself permission to live my life and how I realized it was mostly I holding myself back.

Having trained as a psychotherapist, I am now a life coach and have had the great honour of working with hundreds of people as they build and navigate their lives, but I also started to see a "pattern" or "block" emerge in my clients. They would stop themselves moving forward. They worried so much about what might go wrong that they stalled. The simple act of articulating what they wanted to do, and where they wanted to go, often very quickly removed this block. I also started to see that there was a simple journey most people went on to get to the point that they could dream big for their lives and be at the point that they could instigate all their plans to achieve their goals.

I outline this process in the book and I refer to it as the "Permission Journey." To illustrate some of the life coaching tools and techniques I shared client stories to bring the concepts to life. Many readers seemed to identify with the protagonists and were then able to embark on their own journey with inspiring results. They liked reading about other people's lives. At this point, I created and trademarked the Give YourSelf Permission® Empowerment Programs brand.

So what to do next? My mission in life is to be the catalyst for change. "Be the change you want to see in the world" — loosely attributed to Gandhi. I have worked hard to overcome crippling self-doubt, anxiety and illness and I have had the, often overwhelming, experience of seeing my clients take huge risks and make massive change for themselves. I love coaching, but the world is a big place and there is only so much of me to go around.

In late 2014, I married international publisher (and my high school sweetheart — with a 27 year gap) James Charles Darnborough and he came up with the idea of launching a magazine that would publish other people's stories of where they gave themselves permission. The idea had a few different facets. We wanted to connect with more people worldwide; we wanted to give people who otherwise would not have the opportunity to be published in print a chance to get their writings out; we wanted people to be inspired to empower themselves and we wanted to create a beautiful piece of literature. The latter was achieved with the help of our amazing designer Cathy Henszey and the love and support of many others. This was a brand new venture and many people took a leap of faith in getting involved. With much work, determination and tears, on my part, we were able to publish the Fall 2015 edition of the Give YourSelf Permission Magazine®. It was everything we hoped it would be, and more, and we were so proud of our authors. I call them "our" authors because they took a chance in entrusting us with their stories and I take that responsibility very seriously. I feel the same way for each and every one of the additional Anthology authors.

Very quickly, after the first edition of the magazine came out, we had to start working on the next one. Anybody who has ever worked in periodical publications will know that the pace is relentless and success with a start-up print magazine, these days, is not always on the upward trajectory. We started to receive new submissions but we also wrestled with the idea of stopping the magazine and returning all our subscribers money. It was very difficult for us, but then I received a story that I knew just had to be told. It made me stop dead in my tracks and almost brought me to my knees. It was so honest and poignant that I knew I would go against my purpose in life to not get it published some way and share it with others. I was sure it was going to be able to educate and help many people. Of course, I am not going to tell you which one it is because that would be cheating. You will have your own that will speak to you above all others. Many will stop you in your tracks and some will make you catch your breath, and others will barely strike a chord with you. And, that's ok. We are all different; we have different experiences and relate to different things.

So, with a collection of stories in hand and a business model that regrettably did not make sense, we wondered what to do next. How to get these stories out? The idea for the "Give YourSelf Permission" concept came from a conversation over dinner with friends. As luck would have it, this is also how the idea for the Anthology came about. My lovely friend Leanne said, "Why don't you just put all the stories in a book!" Brilliant idea ... why did I not think of that? I had had the idea to have a series of Give YourSelf Permission books by single authors in their area of expertise (which we are still planning on doing), but never a collection of stories by different authors. Now with modern printing techniques this was completely possible. We were very excited!

Now what to call it? I'm always a big fan of, "It does what it says on the tin," meaning, keep it simple and make it obvious. Knowing that an "anthology" was a collection of short stories that were of the same theme and had mostly been published in a previous publication, I figured we could include the original sixteen stories from the magazine and reach out for more. We were lucky, we had many submissions from people from all walks of life. Some are experts in their field and others are everyday people who have a story to share. But they all shared their story with encompassing grace and love. Our task was now to get the balance right.

At this point I needed help, and the fantastic Nanette Stein answered our call. She has served valiantly and tirelessly as the editor on this book and has been my partner in crime. I always say to my coaching clients that I am their partner in crime, and now it is amazing to have one of my own. One I trust implicitly and get along with very well. We got to work, and this book is the product of that collaboration.

After looking at all the submissions we divided the pieces up into four broad categories: Family and Relationships; Health and Wellness; Career and Purpose and Travel and Lifestyle. They are placed in an order like a record, each story has its place and is designed to flow from one to the next, however, I always think there is value in flipping to a page and reading the story you land on. Let the fates decide, it might be a story you initially thought you might not be interested in, but then it takes a twist and it is just the story you need to read at that time and space. The Universe has a funny way of giving you what you need at exactly the right time. Different stories will resonate with different people at different points in their lives. This is why you can keep coming back to the book and read a different story, or even the same one, just at a different point in your life and have a totally new experience. I dare anyone to not find something that speaks to him or her in one or more of the stories in this book. I may come to regret this challenge, but that is how strongly I believe in our authors and their stories, the human will to survive and our ability to change the course of our life if we so choose.

Each author has worked tirelessly to give you their best work, and I hope you enjoy their stories as much as we do. These are stories I hope help you on this journey of life. Remember, we are all in this together and that is an immense blessing. May we all be each other's confidants and, possibly, partners in crime!

Priya Rana Kapoor,
Creator, *Give YourSelf Permission*° *Anthology*

FAMILY & RELATIONSHIPS

Give YourSelf Permission to Say "I Love You"

by
Heera Kapoor

I had always been a pretty solitary person, independent and even nonchalant. I didn't bother to tell my family all I was doing; I lived my own life. I struggled with the same issues everyone else does: money, work, the daily grind, etc. But I was doing fine, everything being said.

I worked in New York in PR for a software company, and had also just completed my emergency medical technician (EMT) training. I liked EMT work; I always wanted to do something different, learn new things, and help people.

I lived in Brooklyn, so I took the subway to work and came out between my office buildings at One Liberty Plaza and the World Trade Center. I admired the beautiful September morning as I walked into work 15 years ago.

I didn't hear anything at first, but I felt it. The building shook, and through our window that overlooked the Hudson River, dark smoke and hundreds of loose papers flew by. All I could think of was, "What is that?" as all the alarms started going off.

My first instinct was to grab the tiny First Aid kit from my office's kitchen and get downstairs. I took the elevator, I didn't even think of taking the stairs.

The lobby was pure pandemonium. People were screaming and panicking. I made straight for the security desk and told the officer there, "I'm an EMT — do you need me?" He told me to stay right there, but I wasn't about to wait around.

I rushed outside and looked up to see a smoking hole in the side of the World Trade Center's North Tower. I thought, "We got this: it's only a bomb, we'll put it out no problem." I searched around looking for other EMTs.

I had a short-sleeved white shirt on. I had to cover my face because of falling glass from the towers as I ran up Church Street, past people standing frozen at the sight of the burning buildings. Why are these people just standing there? They need to MOVE! I could hear a *boom — boom — boom* coming from the towers.

I stood by an ambulance by the South Tower hoping I could be of help. I heard a very calm male voice saying, "Get in the bus, get in the bus." I looked around but everyone's eyes were still on the burning tower — no one was talking to me. The voice repeated, and I climbed in the back of the ambulance and sat on the bench. Not five seconds later, people rush in. A cop grabs my head and pushes me down, laying his body on top of me. The ambulance shook as debris hit the roof.

Everyone was shouting and screaming as we got out of the ambulance and looked up to see the other tower on fire. I shook my head, wondering, "How on earth did they get another bomb up there?"

Someone close to me said, "I keep hearing thuds," and another exclaimed, "Oh, there goes another one." From the broken windows of the towers, it was raining people. Gruesome doesn't begin to cover it. For a moment all I could do was just stand there with the others, watching figures leap from the windows to their deaths. "Why are they jumping?" I asked. A paramedic replied, "They have no choice. They'd rather jump than burn. They want to control the way they die."

Many had been climbing up that corporate ladder their whole lives — often outwitting each other — and where had it got them? Standing at the edge of a burning building, hand-in-hand with each other, secretaries and bosses alike. They jumped together, now equal in all things.

I realized that they may not have said goodbye to their families that morning. What if they'd been in an argument with a loved one the night before? Or if they just rushed out of the house to get to work? They weren't able to say goodbye to the people they loved before they died. And I thought that if I loved someone, I was going to tell them so. Always. They need to know you love them, even if they don't love you back. These poor souls in front of me were proof enough that no one knows what can happen in life.

When you're standing on the ground looking up at them, you just want to run underneath them and grab them out of the air like Superman. I stepped forward but the paramedic held me back. "You can't save them now — they're already dead." It was so alien to me — trained as an EMT to save lives — and to just stand there helpless.

Tomorrow may never come — the next hour might not even have come for me. I heard military jets flying over, heard the towers creek and crack as they burned, the thuds of bodies, people's screams, and falling glass. All I could think was, "This is it. I'm dead." With that knowledge certain, I said to myself, "You're going to help as many people as you can today. You're going to do whatever you possibly can with your time because you're not going to live beyond this day." It was almost euphoric; I was calm and centered.

I ran into a building where some EMTs had set up their

medical equipment in an attempt to help, but then I heard that voice again telling me to "run" as the noise outside grew louder. I ran out a back exit, stepping out into a world that looked like it was in a nuclear winter. I had trouble breathing, my eyes burned, and everyone kept staring around, looking for something to make sense. It was like in the movies, everything so surreal, people covered in white ash and bleeding. None of us understood that the South Tower had just fallen.

I made my way over to a firefighter approaching the North Tower and asked him if he needed help, but he just wanted to go back in and help find his brothers. I wished him luck. He'd need it.

But then I heard a rumbling like an earthquake. I looked up to see the North Tower's antenna tilt at an angle and stared as the top of the building collapsed on itself, smoke and debris billowing out at the impact.

Police barricade trucks came barreling down the street and I jumped on the side of the vehicle, screaming at them, "GO, GO, GO!" Over my shoulder I could see the tower fully collapse, producing a tsunami of dust, dirt, and debris. Everyone was running as the barricade truck sped away, and we watched helplessly as the cloud enveloped everything behind us.

At another aid station, I watched everyone try to make phone calls on a pay-phone. People lined up down the street to make a call and tell their loved ones they were alive, and that they loved them.

All of a sudden my cell phone rang! It was my sister, Priya.

I picked up the phone, "I'm alive, Priya, I'm alive!"

She then said, in a futile effort to diffuse the gravity of the situation, "Of course you are, you're picking up the telephone."

I cried then, and told her, "No really, I'm alive! I had to run for my life — what happened?"

She said, "They took two airplanes and flew them into the towers."

This was the first time confusion hit me that day. "What do you mean, 'they took two planes'?"

"They hijacked them, Heera, then crashed them into the towers."

"On purpose?!" It was unthinkable.

Dust was up to our ankles, the surrounding buildings still on fire, the rubble that had been the two towers was giving off powerful heat and a smell I'll never forget. Papers littered the ground, and empty shoes stood as reminders that their owners had been blown out of them in the blast. Rubble and ash were strewn over smashed fire engines and broken yellow tape.

How could I have known then how many lives had already been lost and why I still had my own? I hadn't seen a single report, no news of what this was, only hearsay, dust, and my own witness. I wasn't supposed to be alive. I was sure I was going to die down there, by Ground Zero. But there I was, alive, trying to find people to help. But there were very few to help at this point. People were just dead, or they were alive and able to walk away to find help further out. We could only try to recover the bodies. It was like looking at the moon after a war.

As I made my way home, I didn't feel the horror and the confusion of the day. I felt only the dichotomy of clarity in the moment without understanding what was going on. Believing you're dead is rather freeing in that way, the only focus is what you must do exactly in that moment. No fear, no hope, just being and doing.

I went down the next day to see if there was anything I could do. I stood on a steel eye beam 50 feet above the smoking remains looking down at it all. I wore thick boots but I could still feel the heat radiating from underneath me, like holding your hand over a hot barbecue. I watched the search dogs and firefighters dig through the pit of broken metal and concrete, worrying over the heat of their feet as they sifted through the hot rubble in search of the dead.

As the days and weeks went on I was mesmerized by the multitude of flyers that plastered every spare surface in Manhattan. The pictures of the thousands of lost loved ones saddened me. Those falling figures now had names, faces, families and lives … and the vision of them, dead or alive, will forever haunt me.

Seeing all that does change a person, though. I live in LA now, a place with a lot of lost souls, but if I can make one person smile each day, then I'm good. Living my life a day at a time, a moment at a time is now something I just do. I have to, after that.

I was always a solitary person, but I became less so after that experience. I make a point of telling my family I love them, calling it out right before leaving the room or hanging up the phone. I live close to them now, when before I didn't think I'd ever move home again. I will never forget those people holding hands as they looked down from the towers, unable to tell their loved ones how much they cared for them — but I still can. I can still give myself permission to say "I love you."

Heera Kapoor has worked in High Tech PR for many years, including a stint at Hill + Knowlton. After nearly 10 years of running her own business in Tahiti, she returned home to LA to be closer to family and have new experiences.

Give YourSelf Permission
to be at Peace

by
Charles Carroll, Ed.D.

The bonfire burns bright in the soft darkness, sending sparks skyward. The twenty-plus people sit quietly in a circle, taking in the sacredness of the moment. The healing and spiritual energy is strong while the warmth and connection of the group is palpable. I sit in a chair immersed in the moment but alone in my thoughts. This is the last meeting of a wellness and writing workshop in Sedona, Arizona. It's been a wonderful, fun filled and productive four days. Excellent facilitators and writing coaches have done their best to impart the essence of their craft.

Tomorrow I fly home. I don't want to leave the warmth and connection I've found here. The lack of television, minimum Internet connection, the healing classes and the overall environment have lured me into a mental and spiritual place I don't want to relinquish, but I have to. I must prepare my mind to return to my everyday life. That place where, in order to survive from a place of worthiness and well-being, I have to invoke the permission I gave myself long ago. That is, permission to be at peace with myself in a world where I routinely encounter stress based on my identity.

I am an African American man living in a world where explicit bias is largely taboo but implicit bias is alive and well. Although less obvious than explicit bias, implicit bias has the ability to produce the same or even greater levels of destructive stress. Stress that, if left unchecked, could easily rob me of my ability to live a full and productive life. This stress has the ability to create a range of negative feelings ranging from a sense of being invisible or unworthy on one hand or representative of something not quite good or positive on the other. The problem with implicit bias is that the person expressing it may be unaware that they are doing so.

Recent neuroimaging research provides some interesting insight on explicit and implicit bias. The research indicates that the amygdala, a brain structure playing a major role in emotional intelligence, controls our initial reaction to things we see or experience. It creates an awareness of our explicit behavior and since bias is undesirable behavior, we modify our actions so as not to express it. As a result, it allows most people to truly believe that they harbor no bias. However, it is the anterior cingulate cortex along with the dorsolateral prefrontal cortex which is the home of implicit bias. This area of the brain appears to operate on a more learned subconscious level. As a result, individuals expressing implicit bias are generally unaware of their behavior.

Several decades ago, in my 20's, I recognized the impact that implicit bias was having on me and the need to find a way to be at peace in spite of that impact. Prior to that time, I had led a relatively sheltered life with very protective parents. I was an excellent student in high school and had embraced the belief that I could excel at anything that I wanted. After high school, I joined the U.S. Air Force and for the first time in my life I came face to face with implicit bias. The pivotal eye opening moment came when I was passed over for promotion after having been an honor student in technical training and having earned the highest scores on qualification examinations in the history of my aircraft control and warning squadron. My First Sergeant politely informed me that I was next on the list and had there been one more promotion slot available I would have been promoted. I was devastated. How did all of the other guys, many with mediocre records, get ahead of me on the list? After a closer look at the list the answer became obvious. The names of all the African American airmen, along with mine, were clustered at the bottom of the list.

I felt helpless and discouraged. It was only later in college that I realized that I was experiencing the initial stages of learned helplessness. Although, at the time, I didn't have a label for what I was experiencing, I knew that I had to take action. The action had to be two-pronged. I had to actively confront and seek to end bias when and wherever I could; and, I had to find a way to keep bias from robbing me of my personal peace and the ability to excel in life. I quickly realized that my ability to do the former depended heavily on my ability to do the latter.

Shortly after the promotion incident, I received an overseas assignment to South Korea for thirteen months. The assignment was an isolated one and was a blessing in disguise. I was one of 30 airmen assigned to a small radar station on South Korea's eastern coast. Although the assignment deprived me of the support of my family and close friends, the relative isolation gave me time to think and develop strategies to deal with my future. The strategies I developed were never formalized but were based on calming my mind, developing and focusing on goals, and keeping my thought process positive.

During my tour of duty in South Korea, I began studying

meditation and self-hypnosis, both of which have been extremely useful to me. When I returned to the states I was well along with my mental preparation of achieving peace within regardless of my environment. I had clear goals and was well focused. Within six months I managed an early discharge from the Air Force and enrolled in college. By the time I was finished with schooling many years later I had earned a doctorate degree. My career has been successful with most of it spent teaching at the college level and working as a college vice president. I'm confident that I would not have been able to accomplish these things if I had not learned to be at peace with myself.

At one point during my career, a colleague asked me to present a brief graduation speech to a group of "disadvantaged" women that he had facilitated through a nursing assistant program. I had given many speeches to a range of audiences; however, this was the first time I had been asked to speak to a group identified as disadvantaged. I was both intrigued and disturbed by the term "disadvantaged" since it is one often used to express implicit bias. I thought it was harmful to emphasize to the graduates that they were less than advantaged.

Normally such an occasion would have only required that I show up and say a few words about how proud the college was of their success; however, this time I felt the need to prepare a more formal speech. Realizing the graduates had probably heard the word "disadvantaged" repeatedly, I decided to give them a different way of looking at the word. In my speech, I challenged the graduates to change the word to "advantaged" by removing the "dis" and assigning the prefix a new meaning. I instructed them to assign the *D* to mean *determined*, the *I* to mean *intentional*, and the *S* to mean *success*. I assured them that if they applied the formula of "Determined-Intentional-Success" equals "Advantaged" consistently, along with a lot of inner mind work, they would find both peace and personal excellence along with the ability to persevere in the face of any obstacle they might encounter. As I delivered the speech, I realized that I had indeed formalized the approached that I had begun developing decades earlier. I was very happy when several of the students told me years later that the graduation speech had changed their way of thinking as well as their life.

This journey may appear to be one in which I gave myself permission to be "advantaged"; however, for me the key was the permission to be at peace in an environment that was often less than positive for my aspirations. Being at peace afforded me the opportunity to plan and act rather than react to adverse conditions. It allowed me to understand my core values and pursue my life purpose, to excel in spite of challenges I encountered along the way. This state of peace in no way inhibited my commitment to facilitate and insist on change when confronted with situations that demanded such.

In retrospect, giving permission to be at peace with myself was the very best gift that I could have given. It has allowed me to have a full and productive career while affording me the opportunity to remain positive and relatively stress free. It also has allowed me to understand and teach others about explicit and implicit bias and their impact. Implicit bias is alive and well and will likely persist indefinitely. It is a malady that has to be dealt with on a daily basis. I am at peace in spite of it.

Charles Carroll, Ed.D., is a U.S. Air Force veteran and a retired college professor and administrator. He has authored a college textbook and textbook chapters as well as a self-help book, Life is an Inside Job, 2nd Edition *(iUniverse, 2015). Originally from Atlanta, GA, he now lives in Florida with his wife Leigh and dog Mollie. Visit his website at www.lifepotentialsolutions.com.*

Give YourSelf Permission to Leave an Abusive Relationship

by

Dawn Lauren Anderson

As I lay next to my passed-out husband at the end of the day, my mind went through the checklist of things I would need. Knowing I would leave the next morning before dawn soothed me and I easily went to sleep.

As usual, I woke without an alarm — only this time it was much earlier than usual: 2:18 am. I silently crept out of bed; so afraid I would wake him. In the dark, I felt my way around the familiar territory of our bathroom, gathering all those necessities of life — hairbrush, hair dryer, deodorant, and make-up. There were no thoughts in my mind — I just needed to leave. I crept by our open bedroom door to my office. It was more than just an office … it was my space.

Routinely, I kept all my clothes there so I wouldn't disturb my husband when I got up at 4:00 am to get ready for work. I changed out of my nightgown into comfortable sweats. Using the grocery bags I'd placed in the room the previous day, I stuffed my toiletries in one and filled two more with clothes and shoes. My laptop was next. In the dark, I unplugged and packed up all the peripherals — I'm gone for good! The absence of my laptop was the proof that I had left.

Still in the dark with all my bags in my arms and the computer bag draped across my shoulder, I carefully tiptoed downstairs barefoot. I couldn't imagine what would happen if he woke up and found me sneaking out, but I knew it wouldn't be good. I turned on a light far away from the front door where I wouldn't be noticed upstairs. "Oh gosh, I'll need a towel to take a shower at work!" Grabbing another empty bag, I went into the guest bathroom and snatched one off the rail. Next door in the laundry room, I added the clean jeans not-so-absently forgotten there from the last dry cycle.

Now I had more articles than I could carry at once. I lined them up behind the couch like soldiers at attention along the pathway leading to the garage — and escape. As fear mounted I carried the bags, two at a time, and placed them in the trunk of my car.

Before opening the garage door I locked the house door. I felt sweat drip down my back as I settled into the driver's seat and locked the car doors. "What if he heard the garage door opening, and notices that I'm not in bed and comes to look for me?" I quickly looked in the rear-view mirror as I backed down the driveway, too afraid to glance forward as I pressed my car's built-in remote control to close the garage door. I paused and noted the time on the clock: 3:09 am.

As I drove away, I started thinking about what had brought me to this point. Through the years, the warning signs that there was something wrong in my marriage changed from fuzzy messages seen at 60-mph to the clear *slow* and then the *stop* of a road construction flagger. It was my time to put a stop to the abuse.

My husband was a volatile, well-educated Cuban, much different from my quiet, hard-working family who held our anger in check. I told myself his threats to harm his previous wife were just histrionic ranting without any backbone. However, a lot had changed in the past two years. His alcoholism had worsened, his medical marijuana use had escalated, and he had started using prescription steroids. I had seen his alcohol use soar from three beers a day to a whopping 60 beer weekly habit.

His threats and aggression toward neighbors brought police officers to our door many times. It had only been a few weeks since I had stood at my front door and listened to one tell us that the next time he responded to our address, he would be required to charge my husband with harassment. I assured the officer there wouldn't be a next time. As I locked the door, my husband silently turned around from his place at the top of the main floor stairs, walked to the refrigerator and opened a beer.

Luckily, I have a large group of female friends, many from work. One such friend in Human Resources suggested I attend Al-Anon. Al-Anon is a 12-step program for friends and families of problem drinkers and/or addicts. It was easy to find a convenient meeting close to home. I arrived early. Assessing the chair arrangement, I sat where I could easily slip out if I felt uncomfortable. Attendees slowly drifted in, greeting and hugging each other until it was time to begin.

When the first-timers welcome began, I stated my first name, adding that my husband was an alcoholic. Sitting there, listening to other participant stories, I thought, "This is similar to the one-on-one therapy sessions I had — only this is free!" I wondered why it had taken me so long to attend, especially since my husband from my first marriage of 23 years was also an alcoholic.

During the next two meetings, I felt a kinship with the other participants' lives, and opened up a little more about my specific situation. No one told me what to do, but I found that many others had decided to stay with their alcoholic loved ones, using coping skills to separate themselves and live their own lives in self-love. This helped me see that I wasn't a total dolt for living with an alcoholic.

After the second meeting, I talked to the meeting leader who mentioned the book, *Codependent No More* by Melody Beattie (January 1, 1992; 2nd Revised edition; Hazelden). Amazingly, I was already on the last chapter, having received it from another friend. In reading it, I realized that my co-dependent behavior was life-long, enabling me to stay in destructive relationships.

The Al-Anon community was very supportive and comforting, but it was easier to be more specific about my husband's behavior and its effect on me while talking with another close friend at work. I told her about his threats and how he scared me. She said, "I think this is abuse. You may be in danger. Why don't you call our Victim Assistance Unit director and get his opinion?" I was aghast at such a foreign idea, but I trusted her.

Within a week of speaking with him I was in the local spousal abuse center, Denver Safe House, filling out an intake form. How could it be? I answered "yes" to the questions over and over again. The counseling session I experienced the following week gave me even more courage to acknowledge my safety was at risk.

I received the name of a divorce lawyer who gave me free advice by telephone. That prompted me to open a checking account using some of the cash in a joint account. I felt financially safe, but I kept thinking, "How can I leave? How do I do this?" like a broken record in my mind.

Finally, while at a conference on the Sunday afternoon just days before my early morning escape, three friends simultaneously yelled, "You have to leave!" After seeing the anguish on their faces, I made my decision and waited for the right moment. That moment came less than 48 hours later, at

2:18 am on that Tuesday morning.

The ding of my car's low fuel warning brought my attention back to my car. I made a detour to the filling station on the corner. As I pumped the gas in the cool pre-dawn stillness beneath the bright fluorescent lights, I felt oddly warm in my aloneness. I'd really done it. I was starting my journey, my new life.

Turning onto Broadway, I headed toward downtown. The first stoplight was green, the next — also green. Every stoplight was green for the entire 12 miles. I thought, "So this is what it's like to be free. The world is supporting me!" I parked on the street behind my building. As I left the relative safety of my car, I had no idea where I would be that night, but now I felt in control of me. Every avenue was available to me for the first time in my life. I had given myself permission to leave, permission to be free and permission to be me.

Through her essays, Dawn Lauren Anderson shares her life experiences so others may see their own situations from a different perspective, listen to their inner voice, and find their courage. She is retired from the Denver Police Department, enjoying her native plant garden, Dahn yoga, and hiking the Rocky Mountains. Visit Dawn at www.dawnlaurenanderson.com.

Give YourSelf Permission to Say "No"

by
Shemaiah Gonzalez

L ast fall, another mother that I was unacquainted with at my boys' school interrupted a conversation I was having with another parent. She asked if we would volunteer to help at a school function the following week.

I answered her with a cheerful, "No, thank you."

She rolled her eyes and said "Ok then!"

The other parent, a dad, declined as well.

When she left I asked him, "Did I answer her rudely?" not understanding the tone of her response.

"No, not at all. I was sitting here trying to figure out how to get out of it and then I heard you say 'no' so nicely I thought I'd try it, too." We both laughed.

Saying "no" is really hard for a lot of people. It certainly was for me for a long time. Saying "no" was not something I grew up knowing how to do as a talent or some other hidden skill. I spent years helping my parents, sisters and friends in a way that was enabling to them and stifling to my own growth. Every time I started therapy of some sort, the therapist would work with me on learning to say "no." My version began to practice avoidance instead. I avoided people who made me feel uncomfortable or took up too much of my time and emotions. I avoided anyone who asked anything of me to the point that I wasn't giving in my relationships anymore.

It wasn't until I was well into my adulthood, married and in my 30's, that I met a friend who showed me that it was okay to be direct. My husband and I became friends with a neighbor, Chris. We both enjoyed his company and would meet up after work for happy hour or a late night cigar. After a few months of these pleasant interactions, I saw him in our building's mailroom and invited him to go to the Farmers Market the next day.

"No, thank you." he replied.

I was startled and began to look for ways to accommodate him.

"Well, if you are busy tomorrow, we could go Sunday."

He answered, "No, I am not interested. That doesn't sound like fun to me. Please do invite me again if you plan to do something else." he added, grabbed his mail and walked out.

I was a little stunned. I was surprised that he had said "no" to me, knowing very well how much we enjoyed one another's company. Could it be that he really didn't care for Farmers Markets, not me? That is exactly what he said. Similar responses from Chris dazed me as we continued our friendship over the next few years. I began to realize that when my husband and I spent time with him, he really wanted to be there. He really enjoyed us. We knew exactly where we stood with him. It was absolutely refreshing.

As I watched that behavior modeled for me, I wondered if I could do that. Could I say "no" to things I did not want to do and people I did not want to be around?

I thought to myself, "Chris can do that because he is so successful."

One day it clicked, maybe Chris is so successful because he says "no." He does not waste his time and energy where he doesn't want to.

I began to try this on my own. At first it was difficult. I felt so uncomfortable that I nearly visibly cringed when I would say "no" to someone. And my "no's" sounded like a question at first. But the more I did say "no" to events I did not want to attend, invitations I did not want to accept and things I did not want to do the easier it got. I began to ask myself internally each time someone would ask something of me, "Do I want to?" Of course, we all have obligations and duties in life that we don't necessarily want to do but need to. I'm not talking about that. I'm talking about being mindful of what you really want to spend your time and energy on.

As I got better at it, I noticed another level to this saying "no" business. Just like I tried to figure out how to accommodate Chris when he initially told me "no," others would do the same to me. I learned to only give more details if probed. I discovered the less information I gave with my response, the less they would try to accommodate or talk me into it. No one really needs to know why I am not going to do something. The more direct, simple, but kind I am, the more people feel it is probably none of their business to ask me why not. So they don't.

Oh the freedom this gives me! I feel that my life is truly my own. This always frees me up to give and say "yes" to what I really want. This behavior also draws certain types of people to me. Not everyone can take a "no." Not everyone wants to hear "no." Yet, as others see that I stand firm, that I do not waver, they either look for someone else or they respect me.

I have recently become better acquainted with that mom at my boys' school who asked for my help. She has asked again for help since then. Sometimes I have said "yes" and sometimes I have said "no, thank you." I noticed that she doesn't bristle at my "no" anymore. I think she has discovered that I mean what I say and when I say "yes" you can really count on me.

Shemaiah Gonzalez is a freelance writer who holds a B.A. in English Literature and M.A. in Intercultural Ministry. She thrives on moments where storytelling, art, and faith collide. A Los Angeles native, she now lives in Seattle with her husband and their two sons. To learn more, please visit www.shemaiahgonzalez.com.

Give YourSelf Permission
to Believe in Miracles
by
Leanne R. Wood

"You are the whitest human being I have ever met!"
It was true, but not the sort of thing that you normally say to someone when you meet them for the first time. I just couldn't help it. The words had tumbled out of my mouth in a hot second and I started to blush for saying something quite silly.

Unbeknownst to me, I had just met the man I would marry a year and a half later. Thankfully he had a wicked sense of humor and flashed his pure white Canadian skin at me causing us both to chuckle at the absurdity of this first introduction.

I had just arrived in Lausanne from New Zealand and he had arrived from the frozen far north of Canada. We were both attending a six-month training program with a non-profit organization. There was definitely no "love at first sight" but over the next few months we became steadfast friends.

As we departed to go our separate ways at the end of our program, I remember thinking how much I liked Murray. I would really love to see him again. My heart had done a ridiculous skippity-skip thing when he invited me to come and visit him sometime soon, but that seemed impossible. He was heading back to Canada to continue his university studies and I was on my way to Dublin to work with the non-profit. I was living on a shoestring. I could not envisage any way that I could possibly make a trip to Canada anytime soon.

I put it out to the Universe that if I were meant to go and visit him, a way would open up for me to do so. I could wait. I felt sure I was meant to see him again. My faith was such that I believed I would find a way. My inner voice was stirring and I was listening.

A year later, I was visiting a friend who had badly injured her back. In just one week's time she was due to fly to Los Angeles for a three-week trip but she was now bedridden and unable to travel. "Would you like my airline ticket from London to LA?" she asked me. "I know you could stay with my friends there." Was she freaking kidding me?

Buzzing with excitement, out poured my story of wanting to visit Murray in Canada.

"You have three weeks," she said with a twinkle in her eye, "so find a way to get from L.A. to Canada and make it count!"

There were a few major obstacles in my way though. I had only enough money to keep me at my current subsistence level of living and not a spare cent more. I had no credit cards. I would have to find a way to purchase return tickets from Dublin to London and then from LA to Edmonton. Hmmmm… I had just one week to find a solution to these hurdles.

The cheapest way to London was by ferry and bus. It was the afternoon before I needed to take the early morning ferry and I still did not have a way to buy that ticket. As my heart was sinking and I was thinking, not for the first time, that I was crazy, I heard my front door mail slot flap open and shut. I ran down the stairs.

There, on the floor, was an unexpected letter from my

sister. As I tore it open, out fluttered a check for the exact amount I needed for my voyage to London! She had no idea that I needed this money and had never before sent me a check. It was a miracle at the perfect time. I was holding proof in my hands and I realized that there was a Power greater than me working on my behalf. I was on my way to America!

Now I just had to get in contact with Murray and ask him if I was still invited to see him in Canada. Through a series of mishaps, timing issues, relocation on his part and lost phone numbers I had been unable to reach him before I left the UK. However, shortly after I arrived in LA, from a nearby payphone and thanks to international directory inquiries I was breathlessly able to dial Murray's number.

I told him I was in the US and I hoped to get up to see him in the next few days, but wasn't sure how. We both agreed that I needed another miracle. Neither of us had a spare penny to purchase a ticket but somehow I knew I would get to see him soon. We believed it would happen.

A few days later I was sitting on a bus and started chatting to a charming South African woman who was also on vacation.

Something truly miraculous occurred next.

She turned to me and said, "Can I ask you a strange question?"

"Oh no, what was coming?" I thought to myself.

"May I give you some money? I know this is weird and you don't look like you need money, but a friend of mine in South Africa visited me just before I left for this trip and she gave me some American dollars and told me it was for someone that I would meet on my travels. I feel like that person is you."

She held out a big fat envelope stuffed full of dollars for me.

Huge tears welled up in my eyes and rolled down my cheeks as I told her why I needed money. I held her in a massive bear hug that lasted way too long as I sobbed with joy, causing a few eye-rolls from the other passengers on the bus. Inside the envelope was the exact amount that I required to purchase a ticket to Canada! It was a truly staggering realization to me of how we, as mankind, are all connected. I was on my way to see Murray and my excitement level was off the charts!

I ran through the security gates and into his warm embrace. I was all fuzzy inside and couldn't stop jabbering away with delight at seeing him again. We chatted through the night, catching up on the past year.

Once he could get a word in edgewise, Murray reached for my hand and gently said, "Do you think we should get married?"

An orchestra exploded in my head and my heart was ready to rupture with the thrill of what I had just heard.

"Yes, I do!"

We had not even dated and here we were deciding to get married! I had not a moment's hesitation in my decision. This kind, gentle, funny and slightly awkward man was the person I wanted to spend the rest of my life with.

Murray explained to me that he could not afford to buy me an engagement ring at this point. Nonetheless, he wanted us to look at rings so he would know what kind of ring I would like for when the time came. We spent a leisurely romantic afternoon perusing jewelry stores and trying on engagement rings.

Before I departed Canada the following day, Murray wanted to introduce me to some close friends of his. We decided to drop in on them after our visit to the jewelry store.

Our engagement news was shared with much joy and laughter and we were invited to stay for dinner. As we were clearing up the dishes Murray's friend called him aside and I saw them chatting quietly in the corner.

We said our good-byes and got into the car to head back to Edmonton for my flight back to L.A. Surprisingly he pulled right into the jewelry store parking lot. Perplexed I asked why we had come back, and was told that we had a ring to pick up!

Then the next amazing story tumbled from his lips.

That afternoon his friend had a past client visit him at work to settle a long over-due bill. From the moment he received this payment, our friend knew that money was not for him. He had the strongest feeling that when he arrived home there would be someone at his house who he should give the money to. In that quiet huddle in the corner, he gave Murray the money and told him to use it however he needed. Unbelievably, Murray now had exactly the amount he needed in that envelope to buy me my beautiful engagement ring!

I boarded the flight back to L.A. knowing that a string of amazing miracles had occurred to bring Murray and me together.

This quiet and unassuming Canadian giant became my husband a few months later and, after 32 fantastic years, he is still the love of my life.

Our life together has been a full and interesting one, far from normal in many ways. We have definitely found ourselves in some stretching situations, but one thing is constant. We continue to give ourselves permission to believe in miracles and when they occur, my heart overflows with gratitude because they always appear at the very moment that they are needed.

Leanne R. Wood and her husband, Murray, reside in Santa Barbara. They have lived in several countries around the world. The crazy yet powerful story of her adventures is told in her new book The Power of Things Untold. *For more information go to www.leanneRwood.com.*

Give YourSelf Permission to Rise Above the Bully

by

Matt Bunke

I was 11 years old, sitting in the car with my dad. He turned to me and said, "You are a great kid, I couldn't ask for more. But today ... for the first time — I was disappointed in you."

What he didn't know was that two days earlier, I was the small kid running around in gym class. I was the perfect prey. A kid named Mark snuck up behind me, pulled my pants down to my ankles, and then ran out of the gym. I was mortified. I turned red and quickly pulled them up.

What do you do at that point? I didn't run to the teacher or principal, I didn't run home and tell my parents — I didn't know what to do.

I didn't tell anyone. I suppose we do that because we are almost more ashamed that it happened. That embarrassment festered in my head that night. I found myself wanting to get the bully on my side. I mustered up the courage to approach Mark and I said, "I don't want you to ever do that to me again, what do I need to do?" He said, "It's simple ... find someone else and we are good." The cost of acceptance into his one-man club was that I had to "depant" someone else. I had to find my own victim.

I quickly found him: Randy was an easy target. We were in the computer lab and when Randy stood up from his chair, I snuck behind him, just like Mark did to me, and pulled his pants down. Randy was mid-step and as he tried to step forward with his pants around his ankles, he tripped and fell on his face. He started crying.

There I was, standing over this young man, looking down as if he was worthless. I was mighty and he was nothing. I was the bully — and it felt terrible. What had I done? That was not me, or the man I aspired to become. Why do we hurt others to "fit in" even when we know that it is wrong? In that moment, I became what I despised in order to gain acceptance from someone who did not matter.

That night, after our 6th grade chorus concert, Randy's mom tapped my dad on the shoulder. I wanted to hide under the table. She said, "Your son hurt my son today." My dad replied, "I will take care of this. Is your son okay?" My dad just looked at me in silent disappointment, which to me was worse than death. He was a true "alpha male."

In my opinion, an alpha male is someone who is a natural born leader. He builds a tribe and protects his people at all costs. Alpha males are loyal, fair, and vocal. They are strong fathers, partners, sons, friends, and employers. These were traits that made me feel safe, and that, in time, I decided to emulate. Alpha males are often revered as heroes. Most significantly, when we are true to ourselves we become authentic heroes — a concept I put much stock in.

On the way home from the chorus concert my dad said, "I am disappointed in you. Don't ever put me in that situation again. You are going to do bad things. You will continue to make mistakes throughout your life. But when you mess up, you must tell me first. Never make me hear from someone else. I will always be on your side, but never make me feel disappointed like this again."

What he said made a lasting impression on me. I admired him and I knew that I never again wanted to feel the hurt and shame I was feeling in that moment. His "pep talk" was not condemning. He gave me permission to move forward and become the hero of my life.

That day he taught me two important lessons.

Lesson one: Grow up and be accountable for your actions. Trying to deceive others just costs too much. On that day, I made a promise to be honest with my dad. I never want to let him down. This now carries over to everything I do in life.

Lesson two: To hell with peer pressure, trying to be cool also has too high a cost. On that day I set out to become like my father — the authentic hero I needed to be.

I realized that a hero does not try to be liked by everyone but is loved by the few that matter. There are few heroes because it is risky to stand up alone. The hero will rise above the bully and protect their family. I've been the victim and I've been the bully. I wonder if we have all been both? Each day I strive to live like a hero. It is important that I am the best version of myself and the authentic hero of my own life. There is no need to bully anyone to be great.

Once I gave myself permission to be an authentic hero, I made it my mission to find and help those who are vulnerable. I mentor those who are at a crossroad in their life. I teach young men to become more than just full-grown males — they need to become men.

As I write this, we have just found out that we will be blessed with a boy as our first-born. Our wish is to have a healthy child who will become a hero, who will rise above the bully every day. A son who will express himself freely and will protect his friends. I hope that he will give himself permission to be *great*. I will be there every step of the way providing unconditional love and encouragement.

If you are stuck in the mistakes of your past, it is time to give yourself permission to move forward and become the best version of yourself. We can wake up each day and promise to be better than we were yesterday. We all make mistakes but we must recover and make change.

Each day, in every way — give yourself permission to be the authentic hero of your life!

Matt Bunke is married to his high school sweetheart and welcomed their first child in October 2015. They now live in Fort Worth, Texas where he works as a civil engineer and is rewriting his past to change his future. He volunteers at the Boys & Girls Club and serves as a mentor for TEDx youth. Visit Matt at www.authentichero.weebly.com.

Give YourSelf Permission to Choose Yourself

by
Sarah Brandis

This isn't a story of terror, rock bottom and rising from the ashes. This is my account of choosing the unknown over the comfortably uncomfortable.

Our relationship wasn't the unhappiest five years of my life. I had travelled with Brian, seen so many concerts that I lost count of them, and we had fun together. In fact, as all my previous relationships had been a bit on the dramatic side, this time things were refreshingly calm. I was grateful to meet a man that didn't have a drink or anger problem like my ex-husband, and who seemed to enjoy the lack of drama, too.

When we met I was 28 and going through my divorce. I was also applying to universities in an attempt to turn my life around and really start living up to my potential. Dating someone who was fun and successful felt like getting a new role model for my quest to be my best version of myself. He had a great career, was financially stable, and had the self-confidence that I wanted for myself. Honestly, I found him inspiring.

But perhaps this had lulled me into a false sense of security, and even made me a bit of a sitting duck. I would let Brian get away with all kinds of petty relationship misdemeanors. I felt uncomfortable about the way he would casually disrespect me with comments about my failings in life. Often it was something about my poor financial status, followed by him picking up the bill for our meal. But I let all of that go because he wasn't like my exes, and therefore I had gotten lucky this time. I had a "normal" boyfriend for once.

Three years slid by without much drama. However, as I was studying a psychology-based degree at university, I found myself paying more attention to my interactions with Brian and wondering why I was feeling unloved in a seemingly good relationship. I noticed a parent-child pattern between us where I was the powerless and dependent one. Although I was now in my 30's and had normal adult responsibilities like everybody else, I felt strangely inferior to him.

His casual insults snowballed for a while until I reached my tipping point. The final straw was when he put his lazy, unemployed housemate before me. How could a guy that refused to get off the sofa most of the day deserve more of Brian's regard than me? I felt so disrespected that I broke up with him and moved out to stay with a friend.

After a couple of days Brian came to find me and we had an argument to rival any I've ever had in my entire life. With years of pent up frustration pouring out of me, I refused to take him back until he admitted that he had been disrespecting me, which he finally did through gritted teeth. But since I forced that apology out of him, of course, my little victory didn't last long.

On the surface I took him back because he agreed to try harder at treating me like an equal. But beneath the surface, I'm sorry to say, there was more to it for me. I don't have any family around to fall back on when times get tough. So honestly, I was more than a little bit scared to break up with

Brian. I was scared to go it alone. And I think this may be a familiar feeling for many people. It's hard to leave your comfort zone, even when it's not all that comfortable.

And then there was the guilt. He didn't abuse me; in fact he took me on holidays and helped me get through university. From the outside looking in I probably had it all. I even remember one of Brian's friends joking to me that he wished he were Brian's girlfriend! I felt terribly ungrateful that all around me were people telling me I was lucky, but deep down I wanted a way out of our relationship. I didn't really feel like myself anymore, and that was starting to worry me. But ultimately I listened to my fear of being alone, not my gut instinct, and gave the relationship another go.

I graduated from university that summer, which was one of the proudest moments of my life. The end of my student days felt like victory, and I could return to full-time work and pay my own way again. And in my strange dynamic with Brian, this felt like my time to regain some personal power in our relationship.

After a few months of fruitless job searching I was getting frantic. I felt terrible that I still wasn't bringing home much money, and of course I wasn't yet fulfilling my potential either. Brian seemed okay with the rent situation, money wasn't a problem for him, but he did want me to find a suitable graduate job. He also seemed to have some very strong opinions about what my new job should be. I was rather uneasy with this; it felt like our parent-child dyad rearing its ugly head again. He seemed to me like a father figure, telling me what was best. And it felt a lot like what was best for him, too. He wanted me to work in the city with typical nine-to-five hours. He never liked the odd shifts and travel I did for my student job.

When a dream job offer came out of the blue I was elated.

My first thought was, "I can't wait to tell Brian."

But boy did that feeling change when I got home. I expected him to be happy for me. But not only was he not happy, he wasn't open to discussing it either.

"I don't want you to take that job."

That was it. I couldn't get any other sense out of him. It all became ranting and a poisonous atmosphere. This new job was everything I wanted, combining social media marketing with the personal development world, but it came with some compromises; occasional weekend work and some travelling. And this was not acceptable for Brian.

This experience left me wondering if this was the best I could hope for from a relationship; to feel beholden and controlled. I didn't want this. I wanted what I believed other people had, support and consideration.

When the realisation of what I had set myself up for finally sunk in, it was more painful than anything Brian could ever say to me. I hadn't been putting myself first, and by setting that example, I had allowed others to do the same to me too. Not just Brian, but other boyfriends before him.

If it's true that we accept the love we think we deserve, then I wasn't showing myself any love by staying in this situation for so long. I had been so grateful to not be in a "bad" relationship anymore that I hadn't considered the other end of the spectrum. I didn't really know how a good relationship felt, or why I hadn't experienced one before. And I stayed longer than I wanted to out of the fear of not being able to manage alone.

Through some life coaching it turned out that I had a huge sense of unworthiness, and this manifested as being the "pleaser" in all of my relationships. *Since that realisation I've been treating myself the way I would like others to treat me, and in the end it was all about choice.* I chose to take that job, which meant putting my own wishes first. And that job turned out to be even better than I had hoped for. Of course I couldn't have predicted that when I made the decision, so I was choosing the path unknown, but it was mine to choose and I put my faith into it. This meant listening to my gut and pleasing myself, not trying to win approval from anyone else.

Shortly after starting the new job, and riding high on the thrill of choosing my own path, I ended my relationship with Brian for good. No disrespect to Brian, but he walked his path and I needed to walk mine. With the stability of my new salary coming in, I was able to move out of his flat without the same fears I had before. I had found a way to empower myself, and to choose my own future without needing Brian's permission.

Today I still have that same job and I continue to walk my chosen path. I am in a new relationship with someone who genuinely wants me to be happy and respects me for who I am. I chose to allow myself to feel worthy of happiness; and I get the lesson now, it's not selfish to put your needs first.

Sarah Brandis is now a freelance Social Media trainer, content writer and digital marketer in London, UK. A trained life coach and cognitive neuroscience graduate, Sarah's favourite topic to write about is the human mind. Sarah enjoys hiking, biking and all things nature. And of course, blogging about it afterwards. Learn more at www.sarahkbrandis.com.

Give YourSelf Permission
to be Assertive

by
Mary Note Law

A couple of years ago, when I turned 50, I wrote, "I'm still the same kid I always was ..."

The continuity of who I was and how I perceived myself had not shifted. I didn't feel like I had aged despite the rampant cultural messages suggesting that I was past some fanciful prime.

Yet lately, I've recognized that "the same old kid" was still carrying the emotional baggage picked up and toted about as a child. That baggage included the stifling of my needs and wants by repressing my voice.

Non-assertiveness was so inherent in me that I never considered any other way of operating in the world; I assumed that this was my nature. Into adulthood my "personality" continued to impair my authenticity. By college, I began to experience a major backlash of this pattern — failed relationships.

I had roommates whom I came to love as dear friends, yet I kept silent when issues arose. One by one, I came to resent these lovely young women, because I was too inhibited to raise even simple concerns, such as, "If you're going to use my shampoo, would you please replace it with the same brand?" Rather than risk the possibility of hurt feelings, I let resentment build until I was the one who rejected them. I was at the point where I wanted nothing more to do with anyone guilty of such crimes as abusing shampoo privileges!

Fortunately, I recognized the destructive effects of repressing my voice. I resolved to overcome this personality trait so I could have healthier relationships, especially romantic ones.

I enrolled in assertiveness training and practiced this approach over the next few years of dating. Thankfully, when my future husband came along, I'd built a small skill set in self-assertion. The bubble of our relationship gave me a safe place to work with the tools and grow. Keeping this relationship alive mattered so much to me that I was willing to push through the fear of disappointing him, risking rejection, and even the unknown. Having rarely ever stood up for myself I had no idea what might result.

I am now relieved and uplifted to find that rejection does not follow when I raise my concerns. Instead my husband and I tend to lovingly (and often laughingly) discuss our perspectives to find mutual solutions. Who knew?

While my efforts were paying off at home, I continued to lack assertiveness with other personal and professional relationships. As with so many other limiting patterns of behavior in life, we often have to reach breaking point to make change. Eventually, I found myself in a position of compromising my own vision so drastically that I simply could not continue to sacrifice my own needs for the sake of another.

I was asked by a friend to include her in a professional project that I was creating — my first solo project with this particular organization, and the realization of the first step of a big dream of mine. This friend is someone whom I love dearly, and I did not want to disappoint her, so when she asked to be included I immediately fell into the compromise-my-own-preference-for-the-sake-of-another pattern. I agreed to her proposal, inwardly despairing. As the deadline approached, I realized there was another problem — my client was expecting the vision that I had presented to her, not the project that would come with my new co-facilitator. I was in conflict; I was at a place where I was going to have to compromise my professional values to accommodate my friend's request. I had no choice. I would have to break the promise to my friend.

I tried the gentle/hinting approach to release myself from the agreement. It felt like a tennis match; every serve I made was returned with a resounding volley. My friend, with her powerful personality, was not backing down — and that was the greatest gift she could have given me. In order to regain ownership of my project, I would have to dig deep and barrel through my fears of hurting her. I did not want her to feel rejected, especially not by me, but being subtle was not working. I would have to be direct and speak up.

"Meek" me was searching for an outside authority to intervene — to tell my friend she must back out of the plan. Finally a bell went off in my head saying, "Mary, you are 50 years old. It's time to put on your Big Girl Pants and speak your truth!" It was time to have an adult conversation.

I prayed, and then called her to ask her forgiveness, explaining that I needed to be out of this agreement in order to fulfill my commitment to the client. She was not pleased with me. In fact, she was defensive and annoyed. She lashed out and I cringed inside, wanting her to be happy. They didn't warn me about this in assertiveness training! But I had no room to back down, so the volleys continued, until I held strong long enough that the match ended and I was still standing! My original plan had been restored.

In truth, my strength in that moment was driven by my need to be true to my client. Yet holding strong taught me a valuable lesson. I recognized the value of giving myself permission to live assertively for my own sake.

My professional project met and exceeded my expectations. My friendship had a bit of a hiccup, and then returned to normal. Best of all, I found my voice.

This could not have come at a better time, as today I find myself in the position of advocating for my aging mother-in-law. There is no room for people-pleasing when administrators prefer to make decisions based upon dollars and cents over a woman's comfort, happiness and well-being.

Now as I go forward, I bear in mind some of these guidelines from my assertiveness training:

1. Assertion is different from aggression. Aggression attacks the other person. Making another wrong and one's self right does not help resolve the situation. This tends to shut people down and evoke defensiveness. Exercising personal power means standing solidly in one's truth, not bulldozing into a situation and overpowering everyone else involved.

2. Lessening aggression begins with speaking in terms of "I," rather than "You." It means owning one's feelings in response to an event. For instance, in response to my friend's request I might have said, "I really appreciate your asking but I'm not comfortable altering this project. I feel like I need to move forward in the way that I had planned." The onus here is on me and does

not in any way criticize her or her request, yet it does underscore my position with strength and clarity.

3. Speak in terms of specifics, not generalities. "You never listen to me!" is likely to evoke defensiveness. "During dinner, I was trying to tell you how concerned I am about the dog, but I didn't feel like I was heard," indicates a specific event, something for a conversational partner to recall and consider.

I've also come to realize a few things myself. Firstly, I can give myself time to reply. I was not prepared for my friend's request, nor did I know, in that instant, how to deny it, but I did know what I would have preferred in this situation. I could have said, "Let me think about it and get back to you." This would have given me time to construct a "no" in a way that was gracious and loving. When another's request triggers a negative emotion in you, you can take that as a cue. You can take a deep breath, center yourself, and either say "no" or assert your desire for time to consider the request.

Now, I also understand that some people argue in response to challenge. Everyone has an inner child, and some throw tantrums. That does not mean that the child in us has to run. You or I, in our adult awareness, can hold that inner child's hand and stand firm in the face of another's tantrum, just as we would on a playground when kids act up. Eventually arguments cease so why not remain true to ourselves?

I now realize that it is invaluable to give myself permission to assert myself in honoring my own needs and desires. I can allow others to be disappointed, trusting their lives to continue just beautifully. This empowers me to realize my dreams, live my authentic life, and bless the world with my unique contributions, just as the world is blessed when you stand tall and make your unique contributions. I still find myself dipping into the old pattern, but now when I catch myself, I adjust.

Mary Note Law is a spiritual author, artist, educator and healer. She lives in New Jersey with her husband and three talented children. Mary is working on her first book and Chapter one is available free to all subscribers. For more information, please visit www.MaryNoteLaw.com.

Give YourSelf Permission
to Understand Your Friendships

by
Shemaiah Gonzalez

In 2003, I moved back to my hometown of Los Angeles after three years living in Portland, Oregon. I hadn't planned on returning. I also had not planned on falling in love with a childhood friend and getting married. I adored my husband (and still do) but I didn't like the LA heat. But there I was, back in LA.

Navigating new friendships was a challenge for me. I had spent the previous two years in a small and intense grad school community. It was a Christian campus where I think all students were contractually obligated to be friends with each other. Upon my return to LA, I discovered that old friends had moved on with their lives. Some were happy to have me back but time, distance, and my marital status had changed how we related to one another. Even my closest childhood friend, Melissa, and I had difficulty figuring out how to fit our lives together again now that we were back in the same state and both in relationships.

I have always been fortunate enough to be a person who makes friends easily. I began to invite people I met at work, volunteering, or in my loft building for happy hour or coffee.

One neighbor, Donna, and I began a friendship over coffee. We had a thrilling first conversation about our shared experiences of being newly married, new to the area and our shared faith.

I was encouraged, and began to invite her more and more often to dinner, on walks, or for coffee. I quickly noticed that instead of becoming closer, our interactions became more awkward. Our husbands didn't click. We didn't find new activities we enjoyed together. The three topics we had originally connected on seemed to have run their course. The only thing that seemed to work for us was to go grocery shopping together.

At that time, Downtown LA was transitioning from a place that people worked, to a place where they also lived and played. We were there early in that transition and at the time there were no grocery stores. To do your shopping you would have to shop outside of the downtown area. Because of traffic, most downtown residents did this on the weekend. Donna and I both had schedules that allowed us to do this during the week. We carefully scheduled our outings at a time in the middle of the day, in the lull between morning and afternoon rush-hour traffic.

One evening, I lamented the state of my friendships with my husband. I complained specifically about how my friendship with Donna didn't seem to be progressing. In my mind, a friendship started out at point A, when two people first met, and then moved toward point B — best friends. Why weren't Donna and I moving toward this?

Frustrated, I asked my husband, "Is all we are ever going to do is go grocery shopping with each other!?" My husband laughed and said, "How nice to have someone to go grocery shopping with!" I kept complaining about the lack of progress with Donna and he repeated himself, speaking very slowly:

"How nice to have someone to go grocery shopping with." It dawned on me. Even my closest friend, Melissa, would not care to go grocery shopping with me. Who would, really? It is a mundane task, and yes, it is nice to have company while doing it. I realize that I can have different friends to share different experiences with.

This was very freeing for me. Looking at friendship through this lens gave me the freedom to just enjoy friendships. I could see them for what they were, instead of trying to orchestrate them into something they weren't. For me, this meant not trying so hard. I could follow the other's lead instead of trying to lead all the time. I could wait to be invited instead of inviting. This also meant I began to try new things and meet new people, as I let myself enjoy them.

Fast forward to a few more years into my marriage, when my husband and I decided to start a family. It took us a few years, but I was able to get pregnant. When our son was born, I noticed some of my girlfriends who were once so happy for me faded away. By giving myself permission to just enjoy the friendships as they were, I could let them float away for a little while, in the hopes that they might return again in the future. By not trying so hard, I was able to see how, in some instances, my new baby could have been painful for a few friends. I was also able to see that, again in some cases, life and our ideas of fun didn't match up anymore. Sure, I am human and it hurt a little to watch friends fade away, but I was able to have compassion for them, and give them space instead of pushing the issue or the friendship.

One of the ways that I make sure I don't get caught up in old behaviors of leading or pushing a friendship with someone who may not want one (or is fine with the level of friendship we share) is by paying attention. I am aware of the reciprocity in a relationship. I'm not saying I make a list of when I give or make an effort with a friend, but I am aware and intentional. Certainly there are times in a friendship where life circumstances dictate that one has to give more than the other, such as births, deaths and illness. However, I notice when I am spinning to accommodate a person instead of just enjoying them and letting them enjoy me. As silly as it sounds, I put notes on my calendar a couple times a year to remind me to take stock. Who do I call and who never returns my call? Who do I reach out to all the time, but who never reaches out to me first? Where am I always the one reaching out? This shows me where I need to step back a bit and give the friend space to walk towards me or be at the level they are comfortable with.

This viewpoint has helped me enjoy friendships so much more. The reality is that I cannot be friends with everyone with the same level of intensity we had when the friendship was at its strongest. I recognize that. Now I have friends with whom I can talk about our children; those with whom I can talk about matters of Faith and others I can go on a walk with, or just have a five-minute chat at pick up and drop off at the school gates. I have a few I can call when I am feeling down and need to talk about the deep stuff. I also have friends I can meet up with when I am in their city.

Since I moved away from LA, I have missed having a grocery shopping partner in Donna. I have not found someone new to share that activity. I now realize what a gift she was.

Shemaiah Gonzalez is a freelance writer. She is attempting to bring back pearls and aprons to the Stay-at-Home mom culture, but her love of rap music is stifling that dream. She lives in Seattle with her husband and two sons. You can learn more at www.shemaiahgonzalez.com.

Give YourSelf Permission to Have a Happy Relationship

by

Marko Petkovic, M.Sc.

Seven years after my wife and I were married, our second son was born. This was also when I left the corporate world to start my own company. Over the course of the next 20 months, I did very little other than work.

Even though I was working a lot, it seemed everything was going in the right direction. Money was good and I felt successful. I was truly enjoying being free from the corporate hamster wheel. But, with the two new babies — our newly born son and our new company — things started to falter on the home front.

During workdays, I'd come home late and, after the kids had gone to bed, I would work even more. I would take my laptop into the living room where I would often work until the early hours of the morning. Meanwhile, my wife would be on the couch, with eyes half open, watching reality shows until she fell asleep. When I finished working, somewhere around 1:00 or 2:00 am, I'd wake her up and we both would go to bed.

With time my wife started to complain, telling me that we had grown apart. At first, I thought she was exaggerating. I honestly felt that we were not having any more or fewer troubles than the "average couple." Deep inside though, we both knew that this was not how life, or our marriage, was supposed to be.

Slowly but surely we were drifting apart. We complimented each other less and less, until we almost stopped altogether. We were both quick to notice what the other did wrong, and criticism, often disguised as sarcastic remarks, started to creep in. Frequent blaming and calling up past events became the norm for us, and we started to have less genuine fun together, aside from occasional meetings with friends.

Make no mistake, we never stopped caring for each other nor did we stop loving each other, deeply. But, there was a growing feeling of emptiness; a feeling that there was a space between us that was growing wider, and we didn't know what to do to close the gap.

The scary part was, our drifting apart and becoming disconnected wasn't something we could clearly put our finger on. It happened so gradually, it just became our way of life and it took years for us to realize that it was happening. Even then, when we finally became aware that we were not as close as we used to be, it was still emotionally "easier" to dismiss the warning signs that our relationship was in trouble. It was simpler to think "we're fine, this happens to most couples" when we had trouble remembering how we once were.

As it usually happens, the growing disconnect and tension we were experiencing was taking a toll on our kids. It was our youngest son, only 4 years old at the time, who unknowingly pushed us in the right direction.

One day, our young son's kindergarten teacher invited us for a talk. It was a long and sobering conversation. The teacher told us that our son had been acting very aggressively. As we sat there, listening to all the details, we got really scared. Over the next two years we took our son to several different child counsellors. We endured the long, slow and stressful process of waiting for appointments and evaluations, and we were at our lowest point. There were times when we could hardly stand each other; we wondered whether or not our marriage was going to make it. Ultimately, during this period of time hoping for the best and expecting things to get better by themselves (and building thicker and thicker walls around our hearts) my wife proposed a divorce.

The realization of loss of that connection we once had, and the new feeling of emptiness, just crushed me; it crushed both of us. It can take a warrior to his knees, I don't care how strong the man is. And it can take a woman, who is so unbelievably smart and strong, and make her feel like she's nobody.

As is happens, this radical act, made us think. All the reports from child specialists kept coming in and they were all saying: "your child is normal." It all came together and suddenly we became aware that it was not our son who had to be fixed, but us. At the very least, we knew we had to change something. We had to change something drastically. That was also the point when I realized that I wasn't putting my family first. My business and my company were first. Then, it was hard to admit that, but effectively this was the reality. So, with a threat, that we could split and potentially change our lives forever, I decided to do another drastic move — sell the company.

The following year, I was finally able to make a deal to sell my company to my business partner; the company that I had spent years building and that had ultimately kept me away from my family. The good thing is, when I decided to do so, I was "free" again, at least mentally. I decided to devote myself to my children and my marriage for as long as it took for us to regain our peace and stability.

Not surprisingly, with more attention to my family, things started to get back to normal. As my wife saw that I was prepared to do this, she started to show much more empathy to my needs, she opened up and we started talking sincerely.

I took note of when we seemed to only perceive the negative things about each other; how we started to believe what we saw each other doing, how we acted or what we said as ultimate truths about each other. I wanted to change the perception of what we were starting to believe about each other. I wanted to be the catalyst of change in my relationship, so I took the first step.

I started doing something thoughtful for my wife each day: a genuine smile, a hug, a loving touch, or a simple "thank you." I asked myself, "What can I do to make her life better, today?" I also made the conscious decision to put my phone down, turn off the television and carve out 10-15 minutes of intentional time every day for our "how was your day" conversation.

I even started to schedule some dedicated "fun time" for us to spend together at least once a week to learn new things with each other and spend time as a couple. Nothing expensive, really ... the purpose was to just hang out together and discuss our hopes, preferences, desires, dislikes, and fears. It was a great opportunity to encourage each other's dreams. This helped us to really get to know one another's hearts, again.

The most important thing? I didn't expect anything in return and I made it a habit to show my love by example and not by my words, alone. I found that, by doing these things, I now had somebody who worshiped me, so to speak, because she felt worshiped by me.

We had scraped and dug our way out without any professional counselling. We found a way to crumble those walls between us and rediscover the connection we once had (and still have) and, today our love is stronger than it has ever been. During this time, I discovered my passion in applied psychology, in which I'm now licensed, studying how profoundly thoughts and feelings can affect human behaviour.

I am so glad I was able to recognize the cycle we were in and give myself permission to take the first step to having and maintaining a happy relationship. It led me to an exciting new career that allows me to spend ample and meaningful time with my family, and I've gained a new outlook on how I live my life and treat others, especially my lovely wife. I learned that, my truth is not the ultimate truth; and my wife learned that, too.

Proof that, sometimes, everything we go through is worth the effort of taking that first step.

Marko Petkovic, M.Sc., is a best-selling author. He writes for motivated but overwhelmed couples who are struggling to balance their professional work with raising kids and trying to be good partners. He now works and lives with his wife and two sons in Slovenia, right in the middle of Europe. He starts his day early and believes that hope is not a plan. Learn more at www.feelgoodrituals.com.

Give YourSelf Permission to Grieve

by
Nanette Stein

On March 30th 2012 I was nearing a spiritual and physical peak; feeling and living the best I ever had. It was a Friday and I was going to wake up at 3pm from my night job as an Imaging Technologist to start training for my second 5K race. Instead, I was awoken at noon by a phone call. That call was the start of a string of terrible news that would change my life forever.

The call was to tell me that my mother was dead.

Even now, the words are unbelievable to my ears. My vibrant, outgoing, vivacious mother, who just turned 69 at the beginning of the month, was gone. Just like that. She wasn't sick. She wasn't old. She was given too high a dose of medication that resulted in a cardiac arrest. She died alone in her room, suffering from the effects of a heart attack. I had just spoken with her via text two nights before and I hurriedly ended the conversation with her because I was just sitting down to dinner. I was always thinking I didn't have enough time to talk to her about mundane things. How I long for one more phone call from her now.

My mom and I never had what you would call a "smooth" relationship, but we were getting there. We always spent time doing things together, but bickered often. Too often. And, right when we were getting closer, learning from each other and changing things for the better, she was taken from me.

What I am grateful for, though, is that I had been making changes on my own for about four years prior to my mother's death. You see, I used to be a very miserable, unhappy person. I fell into a desperate *hate* of everyone and their "selfish" ways. I started to hate my job, the people around me, my life situation … even myself. I was so lost, I couldn't stand myself. I came across a couple of authors completely by chance while flipping through the television channels one day: Dr. Wayne Dyer, who was promoting his new book *Change Your Thoughts, Change Your Life* and Eckhart Tolle, who was discussing his book *A New Earth*. I was in awe of the loving kindness that emanated from these two men. Never being one to entertain the ideology of "self-help," I ventured out anyway and bought both books. I must say, the concepts within those pages truly changed my life. I feel the most important tenant I learned from the philosophies I read was that, it isn't the "thing" that happens to you that causes you so much pain, but, rather, your reaction to it. When I learned to control my reactions to the pain I was experiencing, I changed my outlook on life.

The work I had been doing on myself prepared me by giving me the peaceful centeredness that I needed to get through my mother's death and for the next wave of bad news. Just three months later in June my husband received a call that his own mother had been killed. She had been washing her car in the driveway at 3:00 in the afternoon and was forced into her car by an unknown assailant and taken. She was 61 years old, married to the love of her life and died at the hands of violence.

I entered round two of grief, funeral planning and being the support system for my husband, Noah, and his family; a devastating reminder of just three months earlier. I hadn't fully recovered or dealt with my own mother's death. I had been keeping myself busy not thinking (and not grieving) while I cared for everyone else. It was, therefore, very easy to continue that role of sturdy nurturer for my in-laws. Once again, I had the distraction I needed to avoid the pain of my loss.

A year later, as everything was just starting to get back to a "normal" rhythm, I received another phone call that my brother had also died. His death was the result of his alcoholism. My sister and I immediately packed a bag and drove from Southwestern Illinois to Milwaukee, Wisconsin to identify his body and clean out his apartment. His apartment was not a reflection of how I thought he would be living, but a staunch reminder of his disease. I had to verify with the landlord that this was, indeed, his place.

The amount of physical and mental work that had to go into the cleaning out of my parent's home and my brother's apartment is unlike anything I have ever been through, just like the string of tragedy that befell my family. I was able to dive right into this work, focusing only on the tasks at hand. This was very convenient for me as someone who was afraid to acknowledge and feel the pain of the reality I was living.

It was unbelievable and had me asking all the "why's" that I could think of. There must have been a reason for all this to be happening. Why me? Why *my* family? What lesson is there to be learned from all of this, if any? I was making myself mad with it all.

The guilt I was harboring was substantial. If only I had started this transformation of forgiveness and love with my mother sooner, we would have been at a better place in our relationship. Why did I have to be so selfish? Why couldn't I understand her better?

There was also ample guilt for my brother and mother-in-law. If only we had taken more trips to Florida to see Noah's mom and dad, made more phone calls, sent more cards. Why couldn't

I take more time for my brother? Been there for him more? Let him know he was loved?

I was letting my guilt overshadow my grief. The thought of letting go and feeling the pain of my loss was insurmountable. The fear I had that I would be destroyed if I allowed the feelings to come was crushing. I knew that there was a process to grieving and, when I looked up the five stages — denial, anger, bargaining, depression and acceptance — I recognized each one. But, I also recognized that I was not living; I was merely getting by.

Grief is a process; one that everyone has to go through individually. Not alone, mind you, but we all have our own way and must trust ourselves to find it. It took a long time for me to allow myself to grieve and let go of the guilty feelings I was holding on to. I think by muddling my mind with guilt and questions, I was doing a very good job keeping the feelings at bay. I was not feeling the pain of grief and, in turn, was not allowing myself to heal. When I was finally ready, I sought out the help I needed, through counseling, to get me to the point where I could accept that all of this had happened. I needed help understanding that it was ok to feel how painful it all was and to learn how to grieve properly. I also had all the support of my family and friends, which was hugely beneficial.

After my mother's death, I read a lot more of Wayne Dyer's books and that lead me to a book called *Dying to be Me* by Anita Moorjani. I found great peace in her accounts of life after death and that peace settled in me. All that work that I had done prior to these great losses prepared me to take each situation as it came. I still grieve. I still feel the loss. I still miss these people in my life every single day, especially my mother. But the peace I decided I *needed* and *wanted* and *gave myself permission to have* made it so much more than a grieving process. It helped me to turn what I was going through into a lesson and to try to find the blessing in it. I know it sounds hard to believe, and maybe even a little selfish. But it is up to us — we can choose how we react to the things that happen in our lives.

It didn't happen overnight, I didn't just wake up one morning and proclaim to the room "Ok, I'm done with this grieving stuff, time to look on the bright side!" It didn't quite work *that* way. I realized I couldn't do everything for everyone or be everything for everyone. I had the right to grieve, too, and to be present for myself. Once I focused in on that, the peace came. I was able to look at my situation and *choose* how I would go on. In other words, I could have chosen to curl up into a ball and never live again, or I could choose to hold the cherished memories of my loved ones close and find the lessons contained in my choosing.

Once I gave myself permission to grieve, I gave myself permission to live. And, as a result, I have used my situation to vow to help others suffering from loss and tragedy. I was given the blessing of peace that carried me through some of the worst times of my life. It only feels right to pay that forward and devote myself to helping others through their own tragedies by sharing of myself openly and honestly. If we could all share like that, imagine the bond and camaraderie we could achieve. I certainly think it would make getting through life a whole lot easier.

Nanette Stein is a freelance writer and editor. After her family faced multiple tragedies, she turned those experiences into lessons to help both herself and others through her writing. She took the leap in November 2015 and "retired" from her career as a Registered Radiographer to pursue her writing full time. She lives in Illinois with her husband and son. Learn more at www.nanettestein.com.

Give YourSelf Permission to Divorce with Grace

by
Pauline Capalbo, Ph.D.

It was a beautiful day in late September. The sun was shining on leaves that were beginning to turn into a colorful pallet of rustic reds and oranges. Autumn was just around the corner. The argument with my husband was the same old song of 15 years. Nothing had changed.

I had stepped onto a spiritual path many years prior to this moment. I grew, healed myself and wanted more from life – and my marriage. Believing I could have a deeper connection to love, passion, life and my vision of service to others, I now needed a partner who could meet me in that space. I had done the work. He tried, but could not get there. We were compatible in many ways, yet the gap between us created an intimate disconnect, and we grew apart. I still loved him, our home, and the safety of what our marriage had come to represent, but God was pointing me in another direction, should I have the courage to follow. This was my third marriage and it was supposed to be my last. Right? My forever guy, until death do us part. What would people think of me should I follow the road less traveled and divorce a good man? Was I crazy? Ungrateful? Stupid? Unrealistic?

The same old argument indicated what the next step would be. In my heart, I knew the outcome was to divorce after 23 years of partnership. I agonized over this knowing. "Why did it have to be this way?" I tearfully asked a friend. I cried daily and pleaded with God to somehow make this partnership work. Wasn't love supposed to be enough? Wasn't love supposed to be the cornerstone of some kind of guarantee? Who would take care of him? Who would take care of me? The future appeared cloudy, yet my faith and trust in how the Universe offers guidance provided me with new-found strength. We began living separate lives, under one roof. At this same time, a friend of 40 years was dying of liver cancer. My world was crumbling into pieces.

At 56 years of age, the divorce proceedings began. I refused to divorce in a hostile way. In honor of a 23 year partnership, my heart could not fight, or financially support, the attorneys who would pit us against each other. My intention was for my spouse and me to win, not the attorneys. The solution was to mediate, with love and understanding. I held the space for a higher way to prevail, and it did. We mediated and settled within two hours.

Preparing my beloved home to be sold was excruciatingly painful. My safe haven, where I felt at one with inner peace and beauty, was to be sold. As a healer, I worked from home and created a sacred healing space for my clients. I put my heart and soul into this home, and now it was time to let it go. I cried as I touched each wall, window, molding, tile and door thanking it for keeping me safe for 17 years. It's possible to fall in love with a home and I was in love with mine. I was letting go of two loves, and it hurt. The old me was dying — it felt as though everything connected to the old self was dying too. A new me was emerging although I had no idea who she was!

It was a long, emotionally and physically intense

transformation. Some days I couldn't physically go on and questioned why I was changing my life so drastically. On those days I asked God to give me physical strength if I was to keep going. The next morning I always felt stronger — a sure sign I was exactly where I should be despite the challenge. Most nights I lay awake wondering what tomorrow would bring. I was often tired and weary. Some days all I did was sit on my neighbor's front stoop and cry. What could she say to comfort me? She cried too, as her life was dramatically affected by my choices. We were like sisters — family, and how would life be not living across the street from each other for comfort, support, and her family's joy of playing with my cats on her front lawn? Life was sad.

Almost two years later, our home was sold. I gave away everything I thought I would not need, including my childhood piano. Physical pain permeated by body and I could not walk. My body was purging, letting go of everything I ever believed in, felt or lived through in the last 23 years of my marriage. I limped to the closing like an old crippled woman, clutching the arm of my ex-husband.

Then, I moved into freedom. Everything I worked for in the last two years, now came to fruition. However, things were going to look worse before they got better. I moved into a rental property in a nearby town. Most rental landlords were not animal friendly. With five cats, I had no choice but to accept this house as the young landlords agreed to allow my five kids, but no more. I felt downgraded, forced into a shabby rental house. It was a big change from what I had been used to. I cried every day.

The house had not been updated since the 1970's. It lacked amenities I was accustomed to such as central air conditioning, baseboard heat, a fireplace, convection ovens, granite countertops, big picturesque windows overlooking a golf course offering beauty from every room in the house, and the landscape of blooming flowers from April to September. The rental kitchen was slimy with cracked counter tops, a stained linoleum floor, outdated wall paper, and worn cabinets. The wooden frame to the back door was rotted and the single pane glass window could be easily broken into. I had no choice but to invest a few thousand dollars of my own money to improve the living conditions in the kitchen or I'd not be able to eat in there. I replaced the back door with one of steel to ensure my safety. The small den area smelled of rotted wood from old knotted wood paneling. Peel and stick tile floor remained dirty and stained despite several attempts to clean them. The ancient oil burner functioned at 75 percent capacity consuming excessive amounts of oil. Every time it kicked on it made a big bang causing a power surge. Lamps that were already turned on during the surge illuminated brightly, then quickly dimmed. I felt like I was on the *Green Mile*. Life was very different now.

Oddly, within a few weeks, my perception changed. The tears stopped. I had stayed in the dark night of the soul long enough. I had processed long and hard my anger, fear, uncertainty, and doubt about what my life would be like. Though I had faith and trust in the Universe, living through the darkness was unavoidable. Transformation happens in the darkest moments.

Slowly, the despondence lifted and I began to feel grateful. I had a roof over my head. Furniture I loved fit into the small rooms and I felt at ease. The childlike faces of my cats looked to me with eyes filled with uncertainty. As a kitty mommy I had to make life okay for them, too. Looking out the kitchen window I realized my backyard was adjacent to woodlands that extended miles along the north shore of Long Island. In that moment, the trees spoke to me. I felt safe, protected and humbled. Mother Earth offered support in all ways. Why did it take a crisis to learn I had always been supported by Life itself? New feelings emerged. I felt empowered, free, independent, and my connection to God strengthened.

Shortly thereafter, my healing practice resumed. New seekers came from referrals of long standing clients. Every day was new and fresh with clear guidance from God. Within a few months I learned of a center where space was available to teach classes. I expanded into the new life. From that moment, life changed quickly. I felt freer than I'd ever been, not because I was no longer married, I love committed partnerships, but because I was expressing a new me, and one whom I was rapidly getting to know.

The new me was different, she was and still is awesome! I love her strength, passion, commitment to herself, and a life that is evident by her courageous choices. She's never looked back with regret. Each day continues to bring her new experiences to learn more about who she is, what she wants, and where she can be of highest service to others. She and I are one. I love me.

Life is a great gift. Follow your heart. Be true to you. Let no fear stop you.

Pauline Capalbo, Ph.D., Energy Healer, Intuitive and Channel of Spirit, in private practice since 1999, has assisted hundreds of clients (local, national, international), children and adults, to take control of their lives by learning to love, heal and empower themselves. Healing and Self-Love are within your reach. Contact Pauline at www.awakeningofthesoul.com.

Give YourSelf Permission
to Feel Vulnerable

by

Maja Hadziomerovic

I was born in Sarajevo, Bosnia and Herzegovina. In 1983 it was called Yugoslavia, a socialist brotherhood, concealing a nationalistic ticking time bomb. Bosnia was the most ethnically diverse republic, and Sarajevo to this day is coined "mini-Jerusalem." In a one-block radius from my family's apartment in the center of old town there is a Catholic cathedral, an Orthodox church, a mosque and a synagogue, and they have been there for centuries.

As Bosnia gained its independence in the early 90's, nationalists from the Serb population of Bosnia wanted to remain with Serbia. With the help of Serbian president, Slobodan Milosevic, they seized much of the weaponry of the Yugoslav National Army and launched an attack on civilian Muslims in Bosnia with the strategic aim of cleansing the land for an ethnically pure, Greater Serbia. The very army that civilians had been paying taxes to, to protect them, was now raping and pillaging. Concentration camps and mass graves returned to Europe for the first time since WWII. Sarajevo, the capital city, was under siege for almost four years — the longest siege in modern warfare. By April 1992, the city was cut off from the world with no food, water, electricity or gas, with grenades and relentless snipers descending upon the city inconveniently built in a valley. I was 9 years old at the time.

Growing up, my parents led an expat lifestyle. Their insatiable curiosity of the world led me to traverse the globe with them before I could walk. All I knew was a life on the move — it defined me and I fully embraced it. As I write this, at the age of 33, I have moved 31 times across three different continents, and have travelled to over 50 different countries. In parallel with a demanding job, I have co-founded a non-profit organization, helped produce a feature-length documentary film, and dedicated most of my energy to other people. I found the relentless pace energizing.

This is a story about how perspective can be gained in the most unusual places — and at the most unexpected moments. I was being positioned to learn a very valuable lesson — to pause and listen. It was a moment of stillness that my body forced on me just long enough to remember a repressed memory from my past. Even though I was shown it when I was 18, it was not until I was 30 that I consciously faced, and processed the memory. Only then was I able to let go of its power over me.

It arrived on a random Tuesday when I was living in Hackettstown, NJ. I had placed a mixed CD into my Walkman, put on my headphones and my trainers, and gone out for a walk in the dry autumn evening. I inhaled the crisp, cool air and felt it fill my lungs — the music transported me away. Thoughts began swirling in my head of the day's events: homework; my crush in school; my sister; my parents … and then, like a shock to the system … it hit me. Out of nowhere, my chest tightened, and I remembered. Flash by flash, like a puzzle, I was recalling scenes and experiences from my childhood. I had been oblivious to their very existence for almost a decade.

I realized I was crying so violently I couldn't inhale. My body was shaking as I curled up in the middle of the road, unable to move. At that moment, as the cold pavement pressed against my wet cheek, I felt everything unravel. I felt excruciating emotional pain. I had lost all control. Once I remembered, I couldn't UN-remember again.

A flashback to Sarajevo, in 1992 — I was 9 years old and the city was under siege. I was used to this "new" normal — living in the cold basement when the shelling was bad, long lines for drinking water, or the taste of powdered milk. I stopped collecting shoes for my Barbie doll and started collecting bullets and shrapnel. I found a way to have fun amidst the chaos.

I was no stranger to packing for a trip or a move, but this day was different. The tension in the air was unnerving. I remember being forbidden to bring toys with me, but I hid one in my underpants anyway. I remember my mom sewing money into the inside of her jeans.

I didn't understand why dad couldn't come with us — he always came with us. I didn't want to go without him. Firmly etched in my memory is the image of his face, blurred through my uncontrollable tears. I put my hand on the gritty bus window and he pressed his on the other side, forcing a smile through his tears.

The harder I fought back my tears, the more they seemed to flow. That was the first time I saw my father crying, and the last I saw of him for the next two and a half years.

I tried to compose myself for my little sister and my mom. I had to be strong for them — and for dad. The bus was overflowing with people in each other's laps, in the aisle and on top of suitcases. It smelled of sweat and was permeated with fear. I heard shelling and screaming, but by now, that was a familiar constant.

Later, we would blow our breath on the windows to fog them up when going through military checkpoints; if they saw how many of us were in that bus, there is no telling what they would do to us.

Hours turned into days that blurred together. "I don't have to pee ... I don't have to pee ..." I kept telling myself.

We crossed the border into Croatia, and all I can remember is eating my first piece of fruit in almost a year. It was a nectarine. It is still the most divine thing I have ever tasted. A kind stranger had slipped a few pieces of fruit through the bus window — though I will never be able to thank her, I am forever grateful to her. Once in the Czech Republic, we were quarantined ... for how long? I don't know ... without a routine, time becomes abstract. But that day, I fell asleep with a full tummy and to the sound of birds chirping instead of bombs exploding. As I slipped into slumber, I tried to recall the last time I had heard a bird chirping.

Over the course of the next two and a half years in the Czech Republic I lived in two different refugee camps.

Being separated from my father during the war and the transition from a war zone to a refugee camp was an experience so painful, that the only way for my mind to cope was to wipe it from memory. It's as if my body chose to release it from a locked chamber when it deemed I was old enough to handle its contents, nine years after having lived through it. After remembering its existence, any time I attempted to tiptoe my way to this painful and confusing new/old memory, I lost all composure.

So, I proceeded with the only strategy that was familiar to me, I ignored it for those 12 years, this time consciously. Not only was the pace of my life at that time dizzying, but I also embodied and embraced a savior identity. I was empathetic towards everyone I met, with one exception: me. With so much to save in the world, there was no time to think about taking care of myself — a mantra I saw no flaw with at the time. Besides, I didn't need any taking care of ... I was defiantly "rock-solid."

I had heard about repressed memories in cases of trauma, it just never occurred to me that I could be keeping down some of my own. Surely that was for the women who had been raped, not just bullied; for the kids who ended up in concentration camps, not refugee camps; for those whose dads had died, not those merely separated from them. I considered myself lucky, and certainly not someone with anything to work through. The thought of having my own trauma was laughable. But, as a wise woman told me a few years ago, there is Trauma with a big "T" and trauma with a little "t." As I processed the meaning of her words, I began to allow for the possibility of my own trauma to enter my conscious realm.

So, for the first time, at the age of 30, I gave myself permission to be vulnerable. The impermeable defensive shell finally cracked, ever so slightly. This initiated a seismic shift that vibrated its way into every corner of my life. The changes I made were gradual, not overnight, but like a ripple effect, they continue on.

It started with me wanting to get re-acquainted with myself. Could my body be trying to tell me something? Who was that girl that always prioritized other people's agendas over her own and who am I today? My whole life, I never paused for long enough to ask myself a poignant question, and certainly not long enough to discover an answer or embrace an emotion. And so, I embarked on the adventure of a lifetime, as I took my insatiable curiosity for the world and turned it onto myself. As I learned to be comfortable with myself and my past, so I became more compassionate and kind towards myself. Interestingly, I noticed that when I was kinder to myself, I was able to help people in a bigger way. I can't control what happens in the world, I can only choose how to react to it and what lessons I take away from it.

I confronted my emotional eating, and started moving and strengthening my body. I made time for sleep, quit smoking, and started flossing, cooking, and meditating. I owned my vulnerabilities and met my long-time partner, changed careers, and I started saying "no" when I was too stretched. The ripple effect continued throughout all my actions, large and small. I realized that, sometimes you have to disconnect from the world a little bit, in order to reconnect with yourself.

I became more fascinated by the human mind, behavior, and the mind-body connection. I now focus on the relationships that are important to me and I enjoy them more. I continue to give a lot of myself to the world, but now I do it more mindfully. My pace, though slower, is not an escape from stillness; rather it is a conscious choice to dive deeper and be comfortable with more vulnerability. I now have the courage to listen to myself and to be kind to myself. I am still on this journey, far from where I know I can be, but light-years ahead of where I was nearly three years ago. And it all started with giving myself permission to pause, remember, and feel vulnerable.

Maja Hadziomerovic now lives in London and works in commercial strategy and deal coaching at a Big Four accountancy firm. She is fascinated by human behavior and enjoys public speaking. Learn about Riders of Hope, her non-profit that works with special needs kids in Bosnia at www.rohbih.org and her documentary film at www.intheshadowofwarfilm.com.

HEALTH & WELLNESS

Give YourSelf Permission
to Meditate

by
Dina Proctor

I don't believe anyone needs to hit rock bottom before they begin their journey toward healing, but for me hitting my lowest emotional point turned out to be a tremendous gift that began my road to transformation. The biggest lesson I learned from navigating the rocky road to healing was to give myself permission to take care of myself — and for me that meant learning to meditate.

Many people I've met say they would love to start a meditation practice, but can't seem to stick to it. They tell me they aren't getting results, that their mind wanders, that they get restless and bored trying to sit still.

Until just a few years ago, that was me too.

I hit an emotional rock bottom (not once, but twice) toward the end of 2008 that landed me in a place desperate for answers. I was in my 20's and was clinically depressed. I'd spent the previous 10 years trying various therapy programs and anti-depressant medications. In addition to this inner work, I thought if I could just manifest the perfect boyfriend; the perfect job; the perfect body, I would feel better. I moved apartments. I changed cities. I upgraded my boyfriends. I bought newer and better cars. I went on diets, I tried cleanses,

I went off sugar, I went back on sugar, I gave up meat, I ate meat, I went high-protein, I went high-carb. You name it, I tried it — all in an effort to try to make myself happy; to fill this gaping hole inside, growing deeper and wider as years and ideas went by with nothing changing.

And the self-help books. Oh, the self-help books! My shelves were lined with them. I would read a little of each one but never had the motivation to immerse myself in their get-happy-quick tips, so nothing ever changed. As months and years wore on my depression worsened and the black hole inside me continued to expand.

After almost 10 years of all of this work — the incessant changes and all the "stuff" I tried to fill myself with, I finally discovered something that really worked; that made me feel better than almost anything; that gave me confidence and made me feel attractive for the first time in my life. This magical solution was alcohol.

As my drinking increased, my concern about the moral fiber of my character decreased. I was becoming someone I didn't recognize. I was stealing money, lying to my friends, waking up next to men I had just met, and drinking at work. I reached the point, after more than two years of constant alcohol in my bloodstream, where I could no longer live with who I had become. This was the moment I began to plan to take my own life.

At this point, and quite unintentionally, I ended up in an addiction recovery program. It took me three months to finally realize I belonged there and to agree to give up drinking and to commit to the program.

That's when meditation snuck in. I found a mentor in the program, Grace, who was willing to help me. She suggested that I sit still and meditate by focusing on my breathing for 20 minutes every morning.

At first I balked at her suggestion. *Meditate?* What exactly does that mean — and more importantly — how on earth is sitting there in a floaty, wistful kind of way going to help with any of this self-hatred and suicidal obsession I was stuck in? And how could it possibly take away the intense physical and emotional compulsion to drink constantly? I rebelled at the thought, but she seemed to expect that.

Grace's response to me was, "If your way was working you wouldn't be here with me right now, you'd be off living your life happily ever after. But here you are, so why don't you try my way for a while?"

Well now, that was a good point. So I agreed to try it her way.

The first morning I set a timer and settled in for my 20 minutes. But after about 30 seconds the craving to drink overwhelmed me and negative thoughts about suicide and self-hatred flared up strongly. I forced myself to endure the inner agony and sit as still as I could as I focused on my breathing. But after only about three minutes, my skin was crawling, I was shaking and sweating uncontrollably, and I physically could not sit still any longer. So I got up, cried a little, and slowly, painfully went about my day.

A couple of hours later it nagged at me that I hadn't completed the entire 20 minutes as Grace had instructed. So I tried to sit down again, setting the timer, and using all of my effort to try and focus on my breathing.

Predictably, after about three minutes the experience again became intolerable and — not being able to stand it any longer — I ended the meditation.

Day after day this went on. Three minutes here, three minutes there. Three minutes was my limit. I thought Grace would be disappointed in my failure to follow her directions, but she was surprisingly encouraging. She told me that whatever I was capable of doing was great.

Slowly, as days turned to weeks, the quality of my three-minute meditations improved. I would look forward to them as a place to quiet my incessant mind chatter, to regain perspective, and to mentally reboot myself. I could see why she told me to do this.

In the perspective I gained during my mini-meditations, I realized that instead of money or a lover, I'd actually been seeking inner peace and a sense of happiness and well-being. I'd been plugging into money, food, men, and booze seeking satisfaction, but they never fit quite right and I'd always needed more and more (and more). But the feeling of peace and inner happiness I felt because of my meditations deeply fulfilled me in a way I'd never experienced before.

The way that I've spent these short bursts of time has gradually changed my attitude toward just about everyone and everything in my life. I've found healing from my addictions (not only to alcohol but food, money and men as well), lost weight easily, transformed my relationships, and experienced profound healing in my body and mind. Little by little, this simple meditation practice steadily brought me to a place of deeply rooted centeredness and freedom.

My meditation practice and my work with Grace transformed — and saved — my life. And it all started when I gave myself permission to try a new way, to open the door to healing, to learn to meditate just three minutes at a time.

I have found a depth of inner peace and self-forgiveness today that brings me a feeling of gratitude for all I went through to get here. Though I wouldn't wish my path on anyone, I am profoundly grateful that I ended up where I am today: happier than I ever thought possible.

Dina Proctor is a life and business coach, and best-selling author of the book Madly Chasing Peace: How I Went from Hell to Happy in Nine Minutes a Day *(Morgan James, 2013). Supported by Jack Canfield, Dina's 3x3 Meditation method is helping thousands to transform their personal and professional lives all over the world. Meet her at www.madlychasingpeace.com.*

Give YourSelf Permission to Overcome Sudden Blindness

by

Yolanda Nava

Permission; why is it that we spend much of our lives looking for permission from others, rather than listening to our own hearts, following our intuition, and walking our own path?

I have been at my best when heeding an internal call to action after witnessing social injustice or the need to break through false stereotypes. At the same time, I have failed to give myself permission to let go of a dysfunctional marriage, slow my hectic pace of long working hours, and to make time for my spiritual life.

This emotional crossroads in my life appeared when I inexplicably experienced eight months of sinus and ear infections that did not respond to on-going treatments of antibiotics and Prednisone. At the time, I was working for Governor Bill Richardson, directing marketing for the New Mexico State Monuments. I loved my work, especially because it allowed me to travel across New Mexico to cultural and historic sites and to engage with diverse groups.

Doctors always considered me a poster child for health. They could not understand why my infections did not respond to medication, and lab tests indicated no serious problems. Thinking all was well medically, I wasn't attentive to my internal dialogue or intuitive awareness that something was off, not only health-wise, but personally as well. I was feeling spiritually disconnected and off my personal mission.

The catalyst for change came with sudden blindness, shortly after leaving the Governor's service on June 30, 2009. My husband and I went to dinner and two days later, after a bout of severe vomiting, I lost sight in my right eye. A month later, sight disappeared in my left for three days. Two days of extensive testing produced no diagnosis.

Concerned about the mysterious blindness, I called a spiritual teacher, who told me, "As you already know, Yolanda, this is an opportunity for your spiritual growth."

Her words were what I needed to give myself permission to learn and grow spiritually, while taking on the challenge of blindness and healing.

I had been a community activist, had a successful career as a broadcast journalist, consultant, and governor's appointee, yet losing my sight over a month's period created an overwhelming challenge.

When fear or anxiety overcame me in the hospital, I recalled the words "Fear is false evidence appearing real." I knew that I had to consciously create a different reality, a new thought pattern. I changed my understanding of fear, anxiety, and pain, and turned my thoughts to healing, health, and wellness to redirect the fear into something positive. My spirit was strong even as my body was waning. Although I did not know it until later, my friend had overheard the doctors say, "It's a good thing we found a diagnosis and treatment. In another week, she would have been dead."

I gave myself permission not to give into the fear, the anger, the doubt, or the belief that blindness is "devastating." For me, it hasn't been. I was committed to my affirmative prayer that I was already at the end of the tunnel, whole, healthy, and sighted. I did not experience self-pity and did not ask, "Why me?" Instead, I asked, "Why blindness? To what am I blind?"

When I returned home, I kept to my former work schedule and added daily exercise. Showered and dressed, I was at my kitchen table by 8:30 am. I worked with mobility teachers, and met with a friend who helped me with my bills and mail. She also served as a coach, and slowly I was back to my normal self.

If blindness didn't test me enough, my marriage fell apart. Moving forward with the divorce had financial repercussions. I suffered multiple losses in the four major areas of life: work, health, relationships, and abundance. At this point I was unemployed, forced out of my home, and required to continue paying half the mortgage. I could have wallowed in the story of being a victim. The rug had been pulled out from under me. I've been blessed by always looking on the bright side and focusing on what actions I can take to transform a situation. I chose to walk a positive path. Fortunately, in October 2010, I was accepted into an eight month-long training at the Colorado Center for the Blind.

Throughout the experience of blindness, I learned valuable lessons. The most devastating circumstances can become the source of determination, strength, and inspire transformative actions. Rather than fall into depression, I chose self-discovery, intuition, and learned from the wisdom of others.

Good can come from even the most tragic circumstances. Passion and commitment to a worthwhile project larger than myself helped me to continue to create the life that I am meant to live. I traveled from Colorado and New Mexico to attend board meetings at Los Angeles Plaza de Cultura y Artes, and I started writing a new book in long-hand.

I have also continued to serve others. In 2012, I was on the steering committee to celebrate the 60th anniversary of the film, *Salt of the Earth*. I initiated a symposium at New Mexico State University and delivered an address in 2014 at Santa Fe Community College during Women's History Month.

Alternative techniques for the disabled are available. I use an audio screen reader for the computer, talking telephone and books, and a color detector to help distinguish clothing colors. There's even a digital pen that helps label spices and files!

I developed a system for finding matching outfits by organizing clothes by color and hanging outfits together. When I shop, I ask for specific colors, for example, bright orange and not pale peach. Finding ways that allow myself to engage fully in life activated resilience, gratitude, and the joy of being alive.

Today, with the exception of being licensed to drive, I have regained the independence I knew while sighted. I practice yoga and aerobic exercises, swim, and I am no longer taking any medication. I shop with the help of store employees, and travel by airplane and train. I have recommitted to my spiritual practices, and returned to my love of cooking and entertaining friends.

I have always believed that we are all given gifts by our creator and have a responsibility to discover our gifts and talents, to develop them, and give them back to the word. The challenge that I face (that all of us face) is to draw from a deep inner well within myself.

When I do this, I connect with something greater than myself and realize who I really am. I tap into that inner source, where everything becomes possible. I am empowered to live my heart's desire, which I know is writing, speaking, and giving back to the world. In taking the actions based on my self-discoveries, intuition, and wisdom, I feel exhilarated, joyful, buoyant, and filled with love, creativity, and purpose.

Also, I have given myself permission to seek out help from others and to be able to accept it. I am an independent and self-motivated person, so this did not come easily. My children, friends, and unexpected human angels provided support and encouragement. Connecting with an Infinite Source reminded me that I am never alone.

Most importantly, I have learned to truly understand the words, "Having eyes, see ye not?" I now realize that while sighted, I was often blind to many things. Now blind, I see with more spiritually discerning eyes.

My journey through blindness radically changed my life and created new challenges. Yes, it's been a major inconvenience, yet the journey has offered extraordinary growth and an abundance of blessings. I appreciate more of my gifts. I know who I am and why I am here. I have given myself permission not to resist the challenges, but to embrace everything as good. I find that in living my life exuberantly, I am inspiring others to do the same.

We do not always know what life will bring. There are no certainties that things will remain the same. I do know, however, that throughout my life, I have always embodied a desire for spiritual growth and healing in all areas of my life. So, even in blindness, I give myself permission to trust my intuition, that inner voice, and to continue to pursue my heart's desires, all of which have brought me to a place of gratitude, joy, and the peace that passes all understanding.

Yolanda Nava is an award-winning veteran broadcast journalist and author of It's All in the Frijoles *(Fireside/Simon& Schuster, 2000.) She was a news reporter, anchor and talk show host on NBC and CBS in Los Angeles and Sacramento. She also hosted a nationally syndicated television magazine, and founded KCMY/TV. Her new book* Journey Through the Dark: How Sudden Blindness Awakened a New Spiritual Vision *will be published in 2016. Learn more at www.YolandaNava.com.*

Give YourSelf Permission to Use Your Voice

by
Michael van Leuken

"Our strength grows out of our weakness."
– Ralph Waldo Emerson

I am really good at stifling my voice, world class in fact. I am the best at not speaking up and of making myself smaller. I don't say these things to chastise myself. I try not to do that anymore. My purpose in stating this is to turn it into a strength — to give myself permission to find my voice. Strength, passion and purpose spring from weakness once we discover and transform it.

I became the small and voiceless child in reaction to early wounding. I don't even know what that wounding was; I'm not sure how much the "not knowing" matters. At least for now, determining what caused this first trauma is not important because working to find out stops me from moving forward. Even though I try, I am unable to recall much from my early childhood. I preferred solitude. I was the quiet child, the poster child for, "still waters run deep," preferring to keep to myself and read. There are isolated memories: huddling in the playground slide for warmth and shelter from the rain;

frequently walking the mile to Kin Canyon with my brothers and spending all day in the forest; a classmate's anger because I wouldn't let him copy my paper; a teacher complimenting my art work but saying I should try to make bigger drawings; and walking the two miles or so to my best friend's house. My mother refused to drive and my father worked long hours so I walked everywhere I wanted to go.

The maintenance of the voiceless child included creating a stutter that gave a handy excuse to be disengaged from the world, to rarely speak, and to largely keep to myself. It was a way to render myself as small and invisible as possible. This stutter was truly a gift as it taught me to carefully consider and plan my words. This careful thought was so I wouldn't stumble over consonants, but it also meant I rarely spoke angry words that I would later wish to retract. I did manage to largely rid myself of the stutter but, even when this impediment was mostly gone, there remained the one who dared not make waves, dared not make his wishes known, and dared not put his needs and desires ahead of any other.

The spark that changed the trajectory of my life was not getting a job I wanted. I interviewed for a position I had already been doing for two years on a temporary basis. It was given to somebody else and, at the time, I believed I deserved it more than the successful candidate. This set off a dark period for me where I withdrew from the world. For several months it felt as if I was walking through a dark tunnel that spiraled ever downward. Throughout this period of time I felt more alone than ever. Every day I prayed to God and the angels to stop this downward spiral so I could at least reach bottom. Eventually, that time came. It was also at this time a colleague told me about a book that started me on a new path.

I learned that my new journey had to be started by *me*. I

was placed at the trailhead but I had to choose whether to step forward or step away. The small act of buying *Into the Vortex* by Abraham Hicks was my first step forward, and each day that I listened to a meditation track was another step forward. I also began writing. At first, I kept those words private but eventually began posting them to a blog. Every day that I wrote was a step further still on my journey. Later, I would equate this part of the journey to laying a foundation. This foundation has proven to be a strong and resilient one.

By paying attention to my behavior and noticing that I am most likely to suppress my voice with my own family I concluded that my early wounding compelled me to never be the cause of strife or harsh words to be spoken. Now that I understand this, I can now feel when words die in my throat and I choose to say nothing or "run away" in some attempt to avoid discord. Observing and catching these moments is important, but not being self-critical is just as crucial. On these occasions it is very tempting to berate myself because of what I did or didn't do — this is a trap I've had to learn not to fall into. Instead, it became important to me to be grateful when I noticed my avoidance. The *noticing* is a step forward. Any negative and demeaning thoughts are steps backward or to the side. However, the path is not always arrow straight. There are still twists, turns, and switchbacks, but all of these little events are learning opportunities.

I started to work on interrupting my negative or anxious thought process by first noticing the damaging behaviour of avoidance (often long after it occurred); this is how I started to recognize my undesired patterns. Then, I had to make a choice: was this a pattern I wanted to hold onto or did I want to let it go? How was I going to change the way I would react when these behaviours and patterns showed themselves again? I often noticed that, even if I did not like that pattern of behaviour, it would still show itself now and then, but I accepted it when it happened and encouraged myself to keep noticing. Soon I began to see that there was less time between the moment I noticed the behaviour and the moment at which I decided to make change. I was getting better at this! As I became more proficient at this recognition/change in action, the space between the two narrowed. I finally got to a point where my reactions were much more appropriate and not so damaging to me and everyone else.

Let me explain further. My wife used to let me know when she believes my hair is getting too long. This used to bother me — a lot. It wasn't like my hair really *was* getting long and yet somehow I was just interpreting this as a personal attack. I was getting upset by her opinion because it didn't match my own … I thought my hair was fine, but couldn't speak up to my own opinion. I used to be able to just shrug it off but then, during that dark period, I was no longer able to do so. I would react angrily and stomp off to a corner. The frightened child in me wanted somebody to come to me and tell me everything was okay, but that never happened.

Eventually, I began noticing that I didn't like how I was *reacting*. When a haircut was mentioned again a couple of months later, I again stormed off. After some time, I again noticed I did not like my response but this time I told myself, "I could have handled that better." There were times I was self-critical but, especially then, I learned it was important to observe instead of piling more negativity on myself. The interval between reacting and noticing continued to narrow until one day my reaction was simply saying out loud, "My hair is okay right now."

Part of the point of this story is that it can often take a long time to notice, and then gradually change, behaviour. It is a slow but gentle process. The noticing is about observing and not judging.

I repeated these steps until I began reacting more appropriately. I celebrated every *little* step. I discovered that, simply reacting by telling myself, "I could have handled that better," was a *huge* step forward.

This is the point I am at now with learning how to use my voice. I recognize the opportunities I let slip by more often. I more than occasionally feel my words hit some kind of barrier in my throat. Sometimes I let the words die there, but now it's more of a conscious decision (not always fully conscious, just more so). Sometimes, I actually massage my Adam's apple in an effort to transfer energy there and unstick the words. So many times I realize that what I am suppressing is minor. I've learned that I overthink. I've learned that I can still unknowingly be transported back to that time long ago where I was wounded by words. I don't want others to suffer as I did, so my words stop. This is the small child who loves so deeply and unconditionally that he wants none to suffer by his deeds.

Transforming weakness to strength begins first by knowing what the weakness is and, if possible, knowing how and when it occurred. If this knowing is not possible, as is my case, it may not matter. Truth be told, this should not be seen as a weakness — it is, instead, an opportunity. Observing how you react and how it might make you smaller is enough to start you on a path to changing your own undesired behaviours. Next are the small steps of correcting your actions. Each time you notice a reaction you don't like, you have the opportunity to change it. Eventually, you will come to understand the way these "weaknesses" actually make you better — they are great opportunities to change and grow. Supposed weaknesses can impart wonderful qualities if you simply begin looking for them. This is how weakness becomes strength. And this is how a voiceless child finds his voice and speaks up for himself without hurting others.

"Growth begins when we begin to accept our own weakness."
— Jean Vanier

Michael van Leuken has been married 29 years and is the father of three adult children. He has lived his whole life in Western Canada and has enjoyed travelling through Canada and parts of the United States and Europe. He has worked in IT for 35 years, in a variety of support jobs.

Give YourSelf Permission
to Thrive

by
Darcy M. Burke, M.B.A.

Heartbreak; that sobering moment when you know your life will never be the same.

The moment in your movie life when you must pause to grieve in order to move forward. The moment you feel a higher power, in my case God, touch your life in ways never imagined. Without true heartbreak, you can't possibly understand love, passion or most of all, yourself.

The worst heartbreak for a parent is when it involves your child. As a parent, a mom, you are supposed to be able to "fix it" — no matter what "it" is. And bad things like birth defects happen to other people, not to me! Goodness no! I took my vitamins, stayed away from the evils of the world, decorated the nursery in pink, bought ballet shoes and waited for my perfect princess to arrive and she did! And then on a fateful fall day in upstate New York, a routine pediatrician appointment changed my life forever. My daughter was diagnosed with a serious and extremely complex brain condition known as hydrocephalus — "water on the brain." At that same appointment, it was determined that she also had a potentially fatal heart defect. She would need brain surgery and heart surgery as soon as possible.

My heart broke in more pieces than I can count, and I was devastated.

Doctors told me not to expect too much; she won't be able to walk, she can't participate in gymnastics nor should she be exposed to anything that could hit or cause further damage to her head. That was twenty-two years ago. She not only walked, but her first steps were a run across the living room. She took dance throughout her childhood and I watched from the audience with pride. She got a scholarship to college, my alma mater, and has worked hard to overcome some serious and severe setbacks. Doctors have a license to practice, but I believe that only God has the ability to heal.

One heart surgery and 34 brain surgeries later, I want to tell you that I gave myself permission not just to survive the diagnosis, but to thrive throughout this journey.

First, I gave myself permission to grieve the loss of expectations and unrealistic parental dreams. She would never win the gold medal in gymnastics at the Olympics (because, of course, every little girl does). Most parents don't have these sobering moments until their children are much older and make their own decisions. But when my dreams were burst so early on in my parenting journey, I cried, I threw things, I was angry with God and the world and that was okay. Grieving comes with heartbreak. It's therapeutic. You can't move forward and dream new dreams until you get past the old and unrealistic ones.

Second, I gave myself permission to throw out all those child development books, charts and schedules. How often do new parents compare milestone achievements as their children grow? In my experience it has been far too often. I knew our milestones would be on our own clock, so why time them? My mother used to say to me all the time, "She is only little once." She was right.

Through this blessing (that came as what first seemed like the worst heartbreak of my life) I got to linger in her childhood a little longer — and that is a priceless gift. For those of you in a similar situation, I encourage you to stop comparing and instead, start enjoying. My ex-husband's family and even some friends used to ask me after her first brain surgery and heart repair if she was "fixed" now. The answer was, "No, she didn't need fixing."

Third, I gave myself permission to forgive myself. This was hard. When bad things happen to good people, especially a child, by nature we need to look for someone or something to blame. I am here to tell you that sometimes, things just happen and there is no one or nothing to blame. At first, I went through every part of my pregnancy, delivery, parenting choices, etc., that I could think of. There must be something that happened that caused this tragedy. But there was nothing, not a sign, an indication or a clue that my beautiful daughter was not "normal." So why me? Why my daughter? The real question was not why me, but why not me?

Fourth, I gave myself permission to leave an abusive marriage and believe in myself again. This may seem like a "no-brainer" but let me tell you, when you live this way, it takes courage to leave. Even more courage to leave with a sick baby — more than most heroes will ever muster. And as I left, new and wonderful doors opened up for me and for my daughter. Courage paid off.

I have spent more time in the hospital holding the hand of my amazing and brave daughter through things most parents can't imagine; it probably tallies into months and years at this point. But while I was there, sleeping in a chair by her bed, I was running organizations or holding executive leadership positions. I was active and volunteering in my community and in my profession. I was getting my M.B.A., developing new programs and services, creating business models — I was thriving and I still am.

I choose each and every day to find the bright side of life and as a result, good things fill my days. Just a few weeks ago, we came home from the hospital after being there over a month. Two brain surgeries in two weeks, an infection and a brain bleed took their toll on both of us. But during that stay we bought a new house and I rekindled my own consulting business. I gave myself permission to thrive in a new and different life.

I took the opportunity for the *pause* in those long days, full of procedures and medical interventions to chat about new dreams, on what kind of life we both really wanted and that is what I am building today. I never pass up an opportunity to tell the people in my life that I love them, which leads to fewer regrets. My daughter is the bravest person I have ever known and she gives me the inspiration to be courageous, to take risks and so far, those risks have paid off far greater than I ever dreamed. We didn't have to settle for anything less just because our journey is different, and neither do you.

I have taught myself to give thanks for the blessings that were disguised as heartbreaking moments and to realize, in those moments of pause, the greatest blessings are about to unfold. Enjoy the silence of those "pause" moments. Pause is not easy to navigate nor get through; your whole world stops and moves in slow motion. In my pause moments, in the silence of my heartbreak all by myself, I imagined a life for my daughter and me that no diagnosis could take away. I imagined that we were not merely scraping by in the valley of pity and sorrow, but we were thriving in ways that no one could have expected. Today we are doing just that. Choose to be happy in spite of the circumstances, and then give yourself permission to thrive.

Darcy M. Burke, M.B.A., is the President and C.E.O. of WaterMark Associates, a business consulting firm. She is heavily involved in emergency response in her community, as well as being an active member of the Temecula Valley Balloon Wine Festival. Ms. Burke and her daughter, Marissa, reside in Canyon Lake, California. Please visit watermartassociates.com for more information.

Give YourSelf Permission to Live Well with a Chronic Illness

by
Fabiana Couto, M.A.

I was diagnosed with type 1 diabetes at the age 13. Life got really difficult back then, but I can now see that the diagnosis was actually a tipping point and the beginning of my personal quest for a more balanced life. It did, however, take me a long time and I endured quite a bit of pain.

The word "balance" has taken on a lot of meaning for me over time, and that is probably because I have spent most of my life feeling out of balance. As I grew up, I always thought I had to constantly neglect my own needs in order to meet other people's needs. I wanted everything and everyone else around me to be balanced first, as they were my priority. I constantly tried to mediate family conflicts and counsel friends, however, I never thought of balancing myself as well. I had no idea what I was doing, nor what it was doing to me.

My lack of self-care was rampant in my teens and early adulthood. I remember being 16-years-old and going out with friends to a nightclub — we danced all night.

When I got back home, I took my shoes off and saw that my foot was bleeding, and I wondered why. My dad looked at me and said, "Fabiana, there is a nail in your shoe. Has it been there all night?" I stopped for a moment feeling a bit confused, and then realized that from the moment I had put the shoes on I could tell there was something poking into my foot. It had bothered me, but I didn't take the time to check it out. It makes me sad to think of this episode as it really does exemplify the state of mind I was living in. I was neglecting both my physical and emotional wellbeing.

Diabetes is a 24/7 condition and it was my body's way of screaming out at me ... telling me to take care of myself and seek balance. It was doing everything it could to get my attention.

Even after my diagnosis, I continued living in the old mode for a long time. I was still taking care of the needs of others whilst neglecting my own. So, my diabetes symptoms got severe and I was constantly experiencing high or low blood sugar and I could never achieve balance and didn't have the energy to go through my day. My body was reflecting the way I was living my life — so much out of balance and constantly going to extremes!

Around age 17, I became very depressed. I put on weight because my diabetes was out of control for which I took very high amounts of insulin. I developed bulimia and also started taking diuretics and laxatives to get rid of that weight. I was in pain and was using these self-destructive ways to regain the balance I craved. I couldn't see that life was pushing me to change. The more I resisted, the more I suffered.

Everything changed for me when I was 26 years old and a coworker told me about a friend of hers who had just passed away in her mid-20's because of uncontrolled diabetes. I remember feeling a lump in my throat and a rush of adrenaline in my entire body when she said what she did and I suddenly realized that I was headed towards the same fate as that young girl.

From that day on, I decided to get myself help! I started working with a multi-functional team. I hired a nutritionist, a psychologist, and asked them to work in partnership with my doctor. I also started reaching out for support from the diabetes community and that was when, at the age of 26, thirteen years after my diagnosis, I first met another person with diabetes, and I realized I was not alone.

Nowadays, I give myself permission to embrace diabetes. I now see it as a blessing instead of a curse. It is a blessing because it made me take care of myself. I have no choice if I want to live. I now take care of my illness as it is a very valuable compass for me. Whenever I am getting out of balance, my body alerts me and I listen to it more often than not.

Today, I am more aware of what brings me balance and wellbeing and what does not. I pay close attention to the dynamics in all aspects of my life, from romantic relationships to my work life, and much in between. I get a great deal of pleasure and centeredness from supporting others, but it is just as important to turn that same level of care onto myself.

I am now stronger and more empowered to make a sustainable and long lasting positive impact on this world. It is my responsibility to offer up the best version of myself.

It is imperative that we stop and listen to our bodies when we are feeling out of balance or are in a challenging situation. We need to also hear and understand what it is telling us. There is true wisdom there!

> *"Pain is inevitable, suffering is optional."*
> — Haruki Murakami

I believe that, when we get stuck in a cycle of suffering, there are lessons to be learned.

Stop, listen and look! You, too, may have a nail in your shoe.

Fabiana Cuoto, M.A., currently lives in Brazil and has a Master's in Psychology. She is also a certified wellness coach and is passionate about improving the quality of life of people living with chronic conditions. Recent appointments include the University of San Francisco, California, and Kaiser Permanente. Please visit: about.me/coachfabiana to learn more.

Give YourSelf Permission
to be Sober

by
Michael James Frizzell

A s I write, I notice the leaves have begun to fall from the trees. I am in Paris, sitting in a cafe, waiting for my colleagues to join me.

The light is magnificent but the wind off the Seine cuts through my overcoat and pierces my heart. I can't help but look back over the last 40-plus years and remember the struggle; how hard life has been, how much it's changed, and how I've exceeded my dreams.

I left home at 17 and joined the Marines. Three years later I got out after two tours in Vietnam. The year was 1969. I survived the War but lost my God and my innocence. I had constant ringing in my ears; I suffered from panic attacks; I had nightmares and couldn't sleep. The only thing that kept me from ending my own life was alcohol.

I discovered the power of drink at 19. A young Marine Lieutenant gave me a spare set of his second lieutenant bars and took me into the officers' club in Da Nang. He ordered a Rum and Coke and I followed suit. When the Rum started to take hold, I thought I had found God. I looked up to the heavens, my hands stopped shaking, and I had a feeling of well-being. I actually thought I could make it. I chased that Dragon for many years. I lived a life of remorse and deep sadness during this period of drinking.

I came home from the War to a country of unrest. I felt ostracized. I enrolled in college; I needed to become as educated as possible. My mother had left the family when I was 15 leaving me and my two younger brothers with my father. He found a new wife immediately. After this, I never felt part of a family. My three years in the Marines and my Vietnam experience pulled me even further away from any connection. I was alone.

I went to school and worked full-time. My drinking was getting worse. Now I needed amphetamines to keep up with my schedule. I rarely slept. I was on a path of destruction. The sadness and shame I felt was pulling me further into the abyss. I dropped out of school and quit my job.

I moved to a beach community and the sound of the ocean helped drown out the constant ringing in my ears but nothing helped my dependence on alcohol. I got a job in a bar and I was starting a marijuana business. I was a mess, without fears or morals. I was out of control.

The inevitable train wreck arrived and I was sentenced to 18 months behind bars from two different busts. It was 1979. I'd married not long before, and they took my wife to jail with me, which almost killed me with guilt. I waived my preliminary hearing so she was cleared immediately.

With an impressive War record and a lot of money for a good legal team I continued the case for a couple of years. In the meantime we had had our daughter, but by this time I had added cocaine to the alcohol problem. Cocaine let me drink for longer periods of time. I never slept.

My wife was losing all respect for me and needed to save herself and our daughter. I remember the day she left. She had my daughter in her arms and I watched her walk up the stairs to the street and out of my life. My neighbor, a Native American screenwriter, was crying while witnessing this. Horrifically, all I felt was relief. Now I could drink and use cocaine without anyone bothering me.

I went from a talented young man and a well-respected Marine to a full-blown alcoholic in a relatively short time. I wasn't 30 years old yet.

I lost my case and would be sentenced in the coming months. I was running out of money. I was evicted from my house and had to give my dog away. The booze and drugs were not helping me at this point ... I cried like a baby. It had been a long time since I felt anything ....

I made my way to the Veteran's Administration (VA) hospital in Westwood and checked into the mental facility. I was being processed when I started to have a panic attack. Without alcohol and cocaine, the world started to crash down on me. I could barely breathe. The thought of being in a mental hospital and facing life sober in the middle of losing my family and my dog, was unbearable. I escaped. I crashed on friends' couches and lived in my car. I told my lawyer I was ready to go to jail. It had been two years since the arrest, without priors, and being a decorated Veteran, the judge only gave me six months with work furlough. I had dodged another bullet. Jail was like a rehab center for me. I got out in four months. It was the first time I had been sober in years.

The day I got out was memorable. My wife agreed to take me back if I didn't drink. My intentions were noble, as they always are with an alcoholic. I walked out of jail into the warm embraces of a friend and his girlfriend. I noticed that getting out of jail was much more festive than going in. They both were full-blown alcoholics and had a blender in the van. They handed me a margarita as I climbed in the back.

Needless to say, I boarded the train south dead drunk. When the conductor barked out my stop, I staggered off the train to my wife's sad eyes. A month later she asked me to leave. I was homeless once again.

The shame of hurting my family had put me into deeper despair, but I needed a job badly. I was introduced to a restaurant owner, a Chicago gangster who didn't seem to mind I had just gotten out of jail. He hired me on the spot and I ended up being the General Manager within three months. I had Carte Blanche in the place, with many perks. Six months later I stared at a .45 pistol in my ocean view apartment contemplating suicide.

I was arrested five more times for alcohol related incidents. I would wake up in the drunk tank and the only reason I never had a DUI was because I had a Purple Heart license plate. I'm so grateful I never killed anyone.

I continued on this downward path for many more years. I was sentenced to another year in jail for my second drug bust. I was married and divorced one more time. Another train wreck.

I went back to sleeping on couches and in my car, but I had joined a beach club when I was married, so I could shower and use the facilities. After tennis I would swim out to the club's raft and think. Thinking was always a problem … but for a homeless drunk I was living pretty well.

I bumped into a member's wife one day on the beach. She knew how I lived — it wasn't easy to hide. She said she wanted to invite me to a meeting she was going to that night. I rarely turn down an invitation from a beautiful woman, so I agreed. Before going to the meeting we met at her house and she told me she had been sober for over a decade. She asked if I wanted to get clean and sober. I told her I had tried many times but always went back to the bottle. I didn't have the strength, and I told her I was different and that she probably shouldn't waste her time. She said if I wanted it badly I could do it. One day at a time.

She was my angel it turns out, and saved my life. It was a 12-step spiritual program that gave me the opportunity to be honest about my life and where I've been. I was able to re-discover the kid that I was before I went off to War, and lost myself and all hope. I learned in the meetings that these people felt a lot like I did. For the first time in a long time I felt that I wasn't alone.

I stayed sober for three years until I was having more panic attacks from my PTSD. The VA prescribed me Xanax. After taking my first Xanax, I was drinking within four days. My life quickly spiraled out of control. I got back in the old business, and was arrested again. My daughter and I had grown closer and now I was going to miss more milestones in her life.

I let so many people down. Most of all, I had let myself down.

Thirty days before reporting to jail I stopped taking the Xanax and drinking. I didn't sleep for several days. It was one of the hardest things I've ever done. I walked into jail sober. I walked out eight months later and have lived a sober, spiritual life one day at a time ever since. It had taken me 11 years to finally surrender and give myself permission to be sober.

There have been some very tough times during my 19 years of sobriety. Many friends and family members have passed away, including one of my best friends and my younger brother to pancreatic cancer. I have remained sober through it all. I was diagnosed with stage 2 breast cancer (because of Agent Orange) three years ago. I am now cancer free.

I live the most extraordinary life now. That lost kid has turned his life around and exceeded his dreams tenfold. By living a sober life, one day at a time, and carrying the message to other alcoholics, anything is possible.

I've written the end of this in Dakar, Senegal — the Western most city in Africa. My team has done amazing work there, educating the African leaders on global warming solutions. We're now ready for the next meeting of the Montreal Protocol, in Dubai, which I will be attending.

Michael James Frizzell has been traveling the world the last 11 years working on Global Warming. When he is home in Santa Barbara, CA, he works with Veterans with war related problems. He is currently working on a book of short stories called Places I've Done Time. *Hollywood is interested in turning his stories into movies.*

Give YourSelf Permission to Ask for Help

by
Avril McDonald, Dip. Ed., FRSA

I was 8 years old when we experienced, what we would later learn was, my first panic attack. We had all piled into a beautiful natural thermal hot pool for a swim with friends and I was just as excited as the other children by the fun we were about to have. Suddenly, though, a funny new feeling came over me and I got a stabbing pain in my chest. My mother remembered putting her hands on my shoulders and my little heart was pounding so hard she feared it might burst right out of my chest.

"I've got to get out, I've got to get out," I cried to her in desperation as I struggled to breathe. I thought I was dying. She got me out and managed to eventually calm me down. We both had no idea what had just happened.

At that time, 35 years ago, there was little to no information about anxiety disorders, or mental health for that matter! I lived in fear of having another "episode" or ever being "out of control," so anything new or different from the daily routine made me extremely nervous. At 15 years old, I woke up one day and felt like I wasn't "here" anymore. It was like I was living in a dream, detached from reality. I called it *feeling*

108

dreamy. I saw various doctors but they all drew the same blanks on what might be wrong with me, so I resigned myself to the fact that this was just the way I was — terrified of life and most likely crazy.

I was awash with relief when years later my sister, who was training to be a nurse, brought home some academic material for me that explained anxiety disorders. I couldn't believe that there were even real *names* for what I experienced. I no longer felt alone. This gave me an insatiable curiosity about the mind/body connection and a passion for learning strategies to try and cope. In time, I discovered techniques on how to do this, such as Neuro-Linguistic Programming, Cognitive Behavioral Therapy, Mindfulness, and Meditation. I found thought leaders like Tony Robins who introduced me to *The Science of Achievement* by Napoleon Hill. Here he outlines the idea that you can pretty much achieve anything you want to in life if you just find someone who's doing it well and ask them for their recipe. I was starting to learn and practice strategies that were not only helping me manage my anxiety, but were also encouraging me to reach my own creative potential.

Although I was afraid of things other people didn't seem to be afraid of, I was never afraid to ask for help so these concepts excited me — and still do! I found that, when I asked for help with integrity, honesty, and passion, it would effortlessly flow to me.

I grew up wanting to be a musician, but my life led me on another path of wonderful things such as becoming a primary school teacher, running tours in the Greek Islands, and learning how to master the corporate game. Although I had barely scraped through mathematics in school, I enjoyed building great business relationships and asked for the help that I needed to gain the skills to eventually become a managing director of a global digital entertainment company.

I had a quiet proud moment with myself the day that I presented to two of the world's most powerful people in publishing, and I realized that I had learned some very valuable things. I learned that *my* leaders didn't actually have all of the answers. What they did seem to have though, was the nerve to be able to sit with *not* knowing the answers, then to go find them. I also learnt that it might never feel like all of the pieces of the puzzle are in the right place to bring ideas to life. The important thing is to just get started and take a few steps — even if they are in the wrong direction. You can learn, tweak, and perfect as you go.

Like many women approaching 40 with children, I started to crave more meaning in what I was spending my time and skills on. My heart was knocking and I feared that if I ignored it, a piece of me would die. Although I had found a lot of creativity in business, it wasn't enough for me. I longed for more. I felt that I now had the skills and experience that I needed to try and transform my own ideas into a reality.

When my daughter had her first nightmare, managing that situation came surprisingly easy to me. I just used a proven Cognitive Behavioral Therapy technique that I'd learnt for myself in dealing with anxiety. I simply re-framed her story for her and it was a "Eureka!" moment for me. It sparked the idea to create characters and stories that might help children manage tough emotions, and reach their highest potential. I saw an opportunity to connect all of my dots — my learnings from my own anxiety, my poetry and creativity, my teaching experience, and my experience in business. I now had a clear vision to create something authentic and beautiful, but I knew I would need others to help me realize it.

Over the long and hard six year journey of bringing my creative vision to life, I asked a lot of people for help. I carefully built and nurtured these precious new connections by helping them in return, as much as I could. I discovered a delightful synchronicity and compounding effect when I then connected some of these like-minded people to each other.

I often struggled with how I could ever repay some of the great thought leaders who had helped me. I was initially in awe of them and they had been so generous with their time and wisdom. I came to realize, however, that they received a lot of joy and satisfaction from playing a part in someone else's creative journey — a journey that resonated with them in some way. I soon realized I could pay that help forward to others.

There were a few people who were not open to helping me when asked. But I came to understand and accept that *if I knock on a door and it doesn't open, it's probably just ... not my door!*

Once in a while, like a see-saw, some of the great heights I am now reaching through my creative expressions can still be instantly thrown down like a lead weight to the ground by my anxiety. Anxiety never really completely leaves me, but it does serve as a valuable reminder. It reminds me of the fears and vulnerabilities that are a part of who I am. It also reminds me of the trust I have in the great love and support that I know exists for all of us — whatever our journey may be. We just have to be brave enough to give ourselves permission to ask for help.

Avril McDonald, Dip. Ed., FRSA, is the author of the Feel Brave Series *(Crown House, 2015) of books (little stories about big feelings for 4-7 year olds) and founder of www.feelbrave.com and the charitable arm www.friendsoffeelbrave.com, which aims to give all children access to tools to help them manage tough emotions. Avril is an ex-Primary School Teacher, Business Woman and a Mum.*

Give YourSelf Permission to Trust Your Instincts

by
Marcus Stone

I was leaving the doctor's consulting room. My hand was on the door handle, closing the door behind me. I hesitated. Something made me stop.

I held my breath. I remember thinking, "Should I go back in? What will the doctor think? Will I look stupid?" I exhaled, pushed the door open again and stepped back into the room. In hindsight, this one small decision, made in a split second, probably saved my life.

This story begins in 2004. I was 37 years old, working in central London for a commercial property practice. It was a high-pressured job and I was generally stressed out. I was dissatisfied with my working life — and I was unhappy. This spilled over into my home life as well. I am married with two children and I never seemed to have the time I longed for in any area of my life. Much of the time, this left me feeling inadequate in all sorts of ways.

At this point, I was already starting to feel that a change was needed in my life. My mum had died of secondary liver cancer the previous year that had metastasized from skin cancer. I had also developed ulcerative colitis a few years previously, which I linked firmly to stress.

My commitment to my work had paid off in career terms, however, as I had recently been promoted to divisional partner at the firm. This meant I now benefited from an annual medical check with the firm's doctor in Harley Street.

On my first visit that autumn, I was put through various checks and was impressed by how easily the doctor seemed to be able to make sure everything was OK. It felt a bit like having an MOT (safety and emissions test) for the body. I recall thinking how odd it was that we generally make sure our cars are regularly serviced, but that when it comes to ourselves, we often trust to luck and are not prepared to invest a small amount time to make sure.

Anyway, I felt comfortable enough to raise one or two concerns. I mentioned to the doctor that I had had an irregular mole on my thigh for a number of years and had never been sure about it. The doctor took a look at it and said he thought it was fine. He suggested taking a sample of the mole (a biopsy) and sending it to the labs to check, just to make sure. A couple of weeks later, I received a call letting me know the result had come back completely clear. I thought no more of it.

Fast forward to the next summer and I was with my family on holiday in Spain, lying on a sun lounger (in the shade) enjoying a beer and reading a book. My wife, Sylvia, leaned over and said, "Look at that mole, are you sure it's OK?" She pointed at the spot on my thigh where I had had the biopsy and I must admit the mole had changed and looked a bit odd. "It's fine," I reassured her, "that is the one I had checked and it came back all clear." Again, I thought no more of it.

In the autumn of that same year, I went back for my second annual medical check. Everything was fine, but as I was leaving, something made me stop. The memory of the conversation with Sylvia in Spain floated into my mind. I could easily have walked away and squashed down the uncertainty that surfaced in me. After all, it was this very doctor who had, only 12 months before, gone to the trouble of taking biopsy and telling me everything about the mole was fine. It would not have been unusual for me to tell myself not to be so stupid and to walk away. This time, I chose not to. I gave myself permission to trust my instinct and I walked back into the room.

The doctor took one look at my mole and said, "I don't like the look of that at all." The next day, I found myself having minor surgery to remove the mole completely, which was then sent away to the lab for examination. Two weeks later, I had an appointment to hear the result. I was feeling fine at that stage, having convinced myself that whatever the result, I would be able to cope. On hearing the news that it was malignant, however, I realised I had been fooling myself. Being told about my chances of survival was a slightly surreal experience and one that I would not recommend if it can be avoided at all.

Following this, I had further surgery and a sentinel lymph node biopsy — everything came back clear from that and I'm pleased to say that nearly 10 years later, I am still here to tell the tale! Looking back now, it feels very clear to me that I nearly closed the door on my life that day. If I had not trusted to instinct and re-opened the door, it would most likely have been at least 12 months before I had the opportunity to check the mole again and that would have been too late.

After this, I gave myself permission to make it clear to my firm that I needed a change. I took six months out and never went back. Change for me since then has been relatively slow, up until the last 12 months, where it has felt rocket fueled. There have been a number of key moments recently where I have trusted myself to make the right decisions and my life looks and feels very different now as a result. I have now found alignment and passion in my new career and I am busy bringing more of that into my life. I have a feeling there is further change ahead and I am happy to trust my instincts to tell me when it is right to move on.

The key that opened the door to all that has followed, however, was that day at the doctor's office, the day I gave myself permission to carry on living.

Marcus Stone is a personal coach, writer, speaker and trainer, and loves working to help facilitate and inspire change. He is also a commercial property consultant and lives with his wife Sylvia and two sons, Will and James, in Surrey, England. He can be contacted through his website at www.marcusstone.com.

Give YourSelf Permission to Dance with the Spirits

by
Valerie McNeal, B.F.A., M.S.

I come from a chaotic and violent alcoholic family and creativity was my salvation from depression and despair. The happiest times in my life were when I lost myself in creative expression. All my fears and worries would vanish as I twirled and danced to music or fell into the bliss of painting colors that flowed from a brush. Time and space would disappear and I felt connected to nature and life itself.

I had a series of medical problems and injuries that no one ever explained to me. When I was 3 I was told I was "uncoordinated" and that my legs did not work properly. Someone suggested dance, so my parents enrolled me in a class lead by a Russian woman who taught ballet like a drill sergeant. I took the classes seriously but didn't understand why I was expected to stay and repeat drills while the others were allowed to go home. The rigorous discipline eventually gained me hard-won, and greatly appreciated, praise and attention from the teachers. Apparently, they decided I had potential performance talent and I was surprised when they selected me to perform a solo on television in the *Little Match Girl*.

Although I quit ballet at 10, these early years of strict, systematic training taught me how to express myself and gave me a structure to find happiness when I felt depressed and hopeless from my difficult home life. Dance gave me a way to leave my negative emotions behind, to feel free of all constraints, and took me to an almost euphoric state of mind and body. I felt absolute bliss; nothing could bother me as long as I could dance and paint.

When I was 27 I was driving to meet friends at a music festival. It was about 8:00 in the morning on Labor Day weekend and I was preoccupied with my love life and perhaps hadn't had enough coffee. I heard a whisper in my ear to "watch out"— a car broadsided me on my left side with the force of an explosion. I found myself hanging out the passenger side of the car with the door open. I fell onto the pavement and blacked out. I woke up in a bed in a hospital emergency ward with people running around me in a great deal of chaos. I looked down at my body covered by a sheet and everything looked fine to me. I asked the nurse if I could go home and she kind of chuckled and said, "You're not going anywhere soon." The nurse came back with the doctor and said I would be there for at least three months because I had a severely fractured pelvis. The doctor calmly showed me what a normal pelvis looked like and then what my x-rays showed. I got the message loud and clear. My whole left side was crushed and my left leg pushed up into the hip socket. I was going to get skeletal traction for at least six weeks and a body cast for six weeks more. They wheeled me into surgery right away and I had no idea what to expect.

When I woke up I felt terrible pain from the steel rods drilled through my left hip and above my left knee. A few days later a man came in, attached weights to pull the bones back into place and I went into shock. They gave me morphine shots every three hours but I stayed in a semi-coma for three weeks. I remember hearing the nurses say twice that I was dying from organ failure from internal bleeding.

I thought I was talking to visitors but everyone tells me I wasn't. Call me crazy, but these little happy spirits and angel things were flying around, sitting on the foot of my bed, telling me I would be fine if I did everything they told me to, that I would not only live but I would run and dance again. They coached me on how to heal my internal organs and it was more work than anything I had ever known.

One day, I came "out of the fog" of shock and the nurses ran over to my bed and said, "Welcome back." I immediately asked someone to bring me my watercolors and some paper and, still lying in bed, I began to paint my experiences.

My surgeon said, "You are a miracle," he'd never seen someone with a fractured pelvis as severe as mine who survived and didn't lose any internal organs. He said everyone with my injuries automatically loses their spleen and often other organs. I could actually still have children. I never told the doctor about my "special helpers." My cousin — a doctor — told me it was morphine hallucinations but I have always had these "special helpers" throughout my difficult childhood. I didn't care who believed me at that point and since my survival defied explanation, neither the hospital staff nor I can describe them in medical terms.

They told me I didn't need the body cast after all and released me after five weeks. The doctors told me their job was over and the rest was up to me. They had no idea if I would walk again. I would need a total hip replacement but they wanted me to wait because of my age — at the time, replacements only lasted about 10 years and, in time, I would have needed more than one.

I arrived at my grandmother's house in a medical van with

a ramp to lower me to the ground in a wheelchair. That was when the shock of my new life hit hard.

Dark depression and a sense of doom overwhelmed and frightened me. I had made it home from the hospital, which was enough to handle. This new image of my future didn't match the image I had for myself. I had always been the girl that twirled at music festivals and laughed at my family when they called me a fool. No one could ever kill my body or spirit as long as I could transcend into the "zone" of pure movement and color. Without that outlet I didn't know how to survive

I sat in my wheelchair, afraid to admit to how terrible and dark my thoughts were. Suddenly, my "little helpers" whispered to me saying "Get up and stand — let's see what still works." I used my walker to get up out of my wheelchair and prop myself up. I thought of my Russian "drill sergeant" ballet teacher. I saw her with her stick tapping out the beat of the music and commanding dance positions. I began to move my shoulders, my arms and my neck. That went well so I tried my lower half, which was pretty much a mess. I was afraid of my new body and didn't know if it would crumble if I moved my legs and back. The left side didn't feel attached to my right side since all the bones from my waist down had been crushed and pulled back into alignment just a few weeks before. I began a daily routine of movement exercises to integrate both sides of my body using yoga and dance for pain control, slowly stretching to music to ease my body a few inches each day. I made very slow but regular progress. On days when the pain was too great to move I would paint. Gradually, I had quite a few completed pieces. I was still registered in college and needed 17 units to graduate on time, so concentrating on classes was a good distraction that kept my mind occupied. Eventually, I taught myself to walk without physical therapy.

After I graduated, I began working in architectural

illustration and drafting firms as an apprentice. The paintings I had done as self-therapy began to sell too, which surprised me. I made my living as an artist and in 1996 I gave birth to a healthy girl and raised her as a single mom.

In 2005 I visited a friend in Mexico and took a salsa dancing class. Although I was a terrible beginner, I loved the music and the fluid movements helped my body to feel better. I came home and continued to dance — badly — for quite a while but was hooked. I continued dancing as often as I could and just worked around the issues of my pain and limited rotation in my left hip. I had pain for days after I danced but I couldn't stop. I found that, as I got better at following my partner and could spin, it had the effect of all my joints clicking into alignment.

I finally did received a total hip replacement, 34 years after my car accident. I had a rough six weeks recovery but, with physical therapy, I found myself completely transformed back to before my injury. I can walk normally and I can now dance without any pain or recovery time. Sometimes I forget how I felt before my total hip replacement and have to remember to be grateful for this journey and for my "special helpers."

Valerie McNeal is a northern California artist in Silicon Valley who makes her living as a muralist and gallery artist for domestic and international clients. She has B.F.A. and an M.S. in Therapeutic Recreation from San Jose State University. She is also the single mother of a lovely daughter. You can find her artwork at www.valeriesart.com.

Give YourSelf Permission to be Vegan

by

Barbara Henszey

I wish I could say my decision to eat vegan was born of some enlightened consciousness. The truth is, I was desperate. Overly committed everywhere, determined to be the best mom to two active toddlers and partner in a high-growth business with my husband, running on fumes was no longer an option. I jumped into a conference promising DIY life retooling, and left willing to try a 30-day vegan challenge. That was over 20 years ago.

On the surface, the scheduling flexibility of a business partnership seemed like a brilliant solution for combining work time and mom time. That made-for-TV fantasy didn't last so long. In reality, I needed to be "on," not just "present," 18 hours a day. New town. New mom. New business. Same old me. Clearly, something wasn't working.

The "Revamp-Your-Life" conference, led by a motivational guru, spanned three days loaded with tools to take charge and build up chunks of physical, mental and emotional muscle. A program combining high-quality nutrition and exercise to achieve boundless energy was part of the mix. No proof, no products to buy. Just a challenge to try the plan for 30 days and judge the results for yourself.

The logic and science, as presented, seemed to make sense. The body expends more energy to chew, digest and metabolize meat and dairy products than plant-based foods. Need more energy? Eat a vegan diet and use the energy you save in other ways. Plus get all the benefits of adding extra vitamins and minerals from fruits and vegetables. The corollary to the eating plan was an aerobic exercise regimen to enhance health and metabolism levels.

It didn't take 30 days. I began jogging during the only free hour of my day, early morning, while the rest of the family still slept. I used a heart monitor set to my aerobic range. Within a couple of weeks, the increase in my energy levels and stamina was astonishing.

Next came the "Now, what do we eat?" challenge and the process of unlearning and relearning the best nutritional research. Coming from a generation schooled in the primacy of a meat-and-dairy based diet, going vegan was a fringy, if not radical move. Unlike today, vegan cookbooks were rare and the Internet nonexistent. Many of the scattered vegetarian restaurants served well intentioned but bland fare, as if looking good and tasting good violated some unspoken rebel code.

This journey came full of surprises and stoked two favorite personal values: fun and learning. I experimented with substitutions to old family recipes and others from classic cookbooks. Some results were delicious and some were all-out belly flops. The pivot point came the day I discovered *The American Vegetarian Cookbook* piled on a table at our local bookstore. I wavered seeing the price tag, an extravagance at the time, but Marilyn Diamond's content turned out to be a revelatory how-to-do-everything vegan that guides me to this day. Her foreword says it all: "Eating should be fun" and "Food should be delicious."

The excitement of working through *The American*

Vegetarian coincided with unexpected benefits. My health improved, dramatically. Since childhood, I suffered from frequent and prolonged, often respiratory, illnesses requiring frequent courses of antibiotics and cough medications.

As a student, the semester predictably ended with a few weeks in bed battling some sort of virus or infection. I handled the make-up exams and papers, and read many books, but missed many coveted roles in performances, plays, and recitals. Over the decades, a number of doctors and specialists tried and failed to diagnose the problem.

Some months after embarking on the vegan and aerobic regime, I counted an unusual streak of good health. Just as striking, I noticed that a casual encounter with someone with a cold didn't jump to me that night or turn into bronchitis a few days later. The changes didn't happen all at once. As my body repaired and grew stronger, illness knocked me out less and less. Somewhere around year five, I ticked off an entire year without even a cold. This was absolutely, truly, and tearfully a lifetime first.

It's the getting something, not the giving up, that opens the door to change. That belief guided my approach to cooking for my sons and husband who were happy omnivores. Our special dinners together couldn't disintegrate into food battles. So I opted for the stealth approach: smaller servings of meat and a larger variety of vegetable, beans, nuts, and whole grains.

The discipline of feeding a family forced me to get better in the kitchen in all sorts of creative ways. I needed a recipe arsenal of great looking, smelling, and tasting dishes that could be prepared quickly and easily. We talked about veganism some, and I shared tofu and tempeh dishes. A favorite memory was the night I served "meatballs" with spaghetti and sauce that fooled 'em all ... until *I* took a bite. My tofu imitation looked, and apparently tasted, like the ground beef version. Now that was fun *and* delicious!

Eating well as a vegan meant looking at food in an altogether different way. Meat eaters don't just eat beef, it's tenderloin or rump roast. Chicken is breast or wings. I began to consider food as combinations of colors, textures and flavors. Cashews became whipped cream and tempeh turned into the (un)chicken salad. The kitchen is my palette and just about anything plant-based and edible only adds to the gusto.

How obvious, in retrospect, that the food we eat is where good health and vibrant living begin. High quality foods spur growth and regeneration, and give our body the strategies to protect us from illness. Today, less than 25 percent of medical schools in the U.S. require even one course in nutrition. For me, good health began simply, in the kitchen, and turned into a delicious journey full of fun and culinary adventure.

Here's one of my fun & easy recipes:

SWEET POTATO AND SPINACH TATAS

Tatas are the perfect on-the-go breakfast or between-meal snack. Like its cousin, the frittata, Tatas are delicious warm, cold, or at room temperature. Unlike traditional muffins, Tatas are light, nutrient rich and easy to digest for those of you who tend to skip breakfast. One or two make a satisfying meal.

1.5 c Sweet Potato, Small dice
2 T Yellow onion, Diced
2 cloves Garlic, Minced
1 T Olive Oil (As needed to cook)
1 Tofu package (Soft or firm, silken is too soft)
1 t Turmeric

1 T Mustard (Whole grain/coarse)
2 T Soy Sauce (Or Tamari)
1.5 c Spinach, Coarse chop, tightly packed
Pinch Salt, To taste
Pepper, A few twists

Preheat oven to 350°

1. Combine tofu, turmeric, mustard, and soy sauce in a food processor and blend until creamy.
2. Very lightly grease 8 spaces in a muffin tin.
3. Heat oil in medium skillet or wok over medium-high burner. Add onion, sweet potato and garlic and cook, stirring occasionally, for 5 minutes, or until onion begins to soften.
4. Add spinach and cook until the leaves wilt, about 2 minutes.
5. In large bowl, mix tofu and vegetables. Season with salt and pepper to taste.
6. Spoon mixture into muffin tin. Prepare tin by brushing a very slight amount of oil in the cups.
7. Bake for 25-30 minutes until top is slightly browned and Tata is firm to the touch.
8. When slightly cooled, run a knife around each Tata and remove. Eat warm, cold, or at room temperature. Extras can be frozen and reheated in oven or microwave.

Yield: 10

Barbara Henszey dreams up new strategies for Mind Over Mango, her digital marketing agency, and new vegan recipes while running her chocolate lab, Chewie, along the beaches in Boca Raton, Florida. She's an Eleanor Roosevelt groupie and a Hamilton (the Broadway musical) fanatic.

CAREER &
PURPOSE

Maj. Terri Gurrola hugs her daughter at
Atlanta Airport on September 11th, 2007.

Give YourSelf Permission
to Live Life on Life's Terms
Interview by
James Darnborough

In over 25 years of publishing I have come across many compelling images, but none more so than that of Army Physician Assistant (PA) Major Terri Gurrola embracing her daughter in Atlanta airport as she returned from a tour of duty in Iraq. As we started compiling stories for the magazine, I remembered that image, and I realized that this woman must have a touching story to tell — and I wanted to tell it.

I reached out to her and was thrilled to get a reply. After researching her story and having the opportunity to talk with her, I knew that I had found a very interesting and kind woman who exemplified the ability to be a devoted and loving parent, at the same time as managing a highly challenging career. She was incredibly gracious in sharing her story with me, and here it is, much of it in her own words.

"My Mom locked herself in her room and cried for three days when I signed up." Gurrola explains. "It was 1985 and back then my family was struggling so it seemed like a good route to a college degree." She ended up receiving a bachelor's in psychology, a bachelor's in the military physician assistant program, and later, a master's in emergency medicine.

The US was not involved in any major conflicts the day Gurrola enlisted. There was no way she could have known that she would eventually be deployed to war-ravaged areas such as Sarajevo, Bosnia, and Iraq in both Gulf wars. She would have numerous other postings around the world over the course of her 30 years in the army.

Just like in many war movies or TV series, the medic/PA is embedded with troops out in the field and administers on-site emergency aid. It takes a certain type of individual to be able to do this.

As Gurrola shared more with me about her long career in the service, it became clear that every day that she went to work she required unlimited selfless courage. Often, Gurrola would put her own wellbeing in harm's way so that she could save lives and make a difference in the lives of her charges. The kind of difference her grandfather made as a Navy corpsman, who was also a PA.

"I loved what my grandfather did and knew early on that I would be proud to follow in his footsteps helping our troops to heal their broken bodies, and rebuild their futures," Gurrola reminisces.

Gurrola has been involved in her share of air assaults, foot patrols, and ground missions. Not the sort of thing that was easily juggled while raising her children; Gabrielle, soon to be 12, and Jorge who is 8.

I ask Gurrola about the picture. "Leaving my daughter behind was the hardest thing I had ever done," Gurrola explains. "Gabrielle was going to turn 3 while I was away, and I wouldn't even be able to see her on her birthday. This was in the days before Internet video calls. My biggest fear was that she would forget who I was. I can remember the moment in this picture as if it happened yesterday. It was September 11th, 2007, and I was flying into Atlanta from Iraq for my mid-tour break. I was a captain then as well as a medic, which I still am. I'd been stationed in a place called Combat Out Post (COP) Cleary. Being out there was difficult, not only because I was missing my daughter terribly, but also because I was the only woman on the entire COP.

When I got off the tram from the runway, a gentleman from the USO, the nonprofit organization that works with the uniformed services, came forward to greet me. They do this with all returning servicemen and women. He put out his hand and said, 'Welcome home, Captain.' I knew that my husband George (we've since divorced) and Gabby would be waiting for me somewhere. And sure enough, just as I reached to shake the USO man's hand, I heard this beautiful, familiar voice shouting, 'MOMMY!'

All I could do was zone to the left, where the voice was coming from, and run across the airport. I remember sliding on my knees and grabbing Gabby; I couldn't let go of her for one second. She kept saying, 'Mommy, I missed you.'

I was crying tears of joy for the fact that Gabby hadn't forgotten me. When I finally came up for air, I saw that every single person in that airport was crying, too. Men, women — I kid you not — they were all just bawling."

"How do you feel when you see this photo now?"

"Seeing this picture re-enforces in my heart how important my children are to me and that I should consider retiring." Just two short weeks after this picture was taken, Gurrola was back in Iraq.

"Can you describe some of the challenges you face with your work?"

"I can take you back to July 2007. I was on Forward Observation Base (FOB) Hammer in Iraq and our base was hit with multiple rockets. We suffered many casualties and amongst them, a soldier I'll call Ray, was seriously injured. He was young, maybe 22 (the same age I was when I entered the army) and was lying in his cot when the rockets hit. It took the left side of his face off, including his eye. The bleeding was excessive and I had serious doubts that he would make it. I remember the brigade commander standing by me and asking me, 'Doc, what can I do to help you?' COL Wayne Grigsby was an excellent brigade commander and I truly looked up to his leadership. He helped me several times when Ray would become agitated and pull out his IV.

I worked on the young soldier and knew if we didn't get him evacuated to a surgeon, he wouldn't make it. I also knew I couldn't leave his side. I kept talking to him in his ear.

'Ray, calm down, you're going to be OK.' Every time I spoke to him in a soft, soothing voice, he would calm down. Because of his injuries, there wasn't much to intubate. I kept his airway open with continuous suctioning, keeping a surgical airway nearby, just in case I needed it. I then escorted him to the landing zone for evacuation.

In the end, I realized that what I did saved this soldier. He was able to go home, unlike many others who were not so lucky that day. For years I worried; did I do everything I could? Could I have done something differently? And the bottom line was, it didn't matter, because I did all that I could and he did survive. That is what I was sent to Iraq to do, that's my job. It's the ones that don't make it that tend to haunt me. I have now given myself permission to let go of the ones I couldn't save and be thankful and proud of the ones I have saved. I love what I do and I swear there is nothing greater in life than serving the bravest warriors in the world!"

"You were the only woman in your outpost. How did this affect you as both a soldier and a mother?"

"Everything the guys did, I did. I never turned down a mission. I always gave everything I had to save each life that was brought to me. I always did everything I could to be the mother I had hoped to be be. I haven't yet been able to choose one role over the other. I guess along the way, I've had to learn to live life on life's terms."

After Gurrola's second tour in Iraq, she returned to Fort Benning, Georgia for two years and had her son, Jorge. What is not public knowledge is that she hid her pregnancy for a time upon returning to the brigade for fear that she would not be allowed to complete her tour. Time and time again, Major Gurrola placed the safety and lives of her brigade first. Eventually, she was sent home by the brigade Commander to prepare for 3,500 soldiers to return and to complete their medical assessments. In 2012 she moved with her children to Korea where they went to school and she headed up the medical clinic at Camp Humphreys near Pyeongtaek.

"How is life for you now that you can be with your children each day?"

"I love having my children with me. I do my job and then go home and look after my family," she explains. "I never want to be away from them."

Now, as a family back again in Fort Benning, Jorge is becoming quite an expert at Taekwondo and Jujitsu and Gabby is a natural dancer. Jet skiing and wake boarding on the lake are all part of family life these days.

"How does your mom feel now, three decades after your decision to enlist?"

"My mom is really proud of where I am now. She's actually the first to tell me, 'Don't retire, this is who you are.'"

In closing, I ask, *"What do you think the future holds for you?"*

"I would like to think that after all is said and done, that the future will be good, filled with health, love, and time spent watching my children grow each day into incredible, beautiful, healthy, productive adults. I feel comfortable that they are on that path of success."

Born and raised in London, England, James Darnborough now lives and works in Santa Barbara, California having spent over 25 years in the media business in the UK, South Africa, Australia and the USA. He is the Publisher of Give YourSelf Permission® – Anthology.

Give YourSelf Permission to Chase Green Dots

By
Robyn Geddes

When it came to giving myself permission to pursue art, there was probably no choice in the matter. Growing up in a household where taste was everything, I knew nothing else.

My art teachers from the fourth grade up told me what my calling would be. So, in the mid-sixties when I ventured off to the Museum of Modern Art — that was it. For unknown reasons, I was drawn right to the surface of a group of large paintings from Japan, green brush strokes silk-screened on white ground.

Even though I had no idea what was in front of me, the green dots fascinated me. Over the ensuing years, I dabbled in painting and, when the time came to think about a career, I can still remember my parents saying, "You do not want to be an artist. You will end up broke and miserable."

Economic hardship and dead-end jobs followed my parent's sound advice. Fortunately, I was able to land many good jobs, starting with Andy Warhol's factory. And with exposure, came other avenues of fascination — more green dots to chase.

Over the years, those green dots have included everything that caught my eye. Whether it was cardboard or cement, detailed or haphazard — if it caught my imagination, then nothing else mattered.

California-based Robyn Geddes started his career working at Andy Warhol's factory from 1978 to 1983. He went on to work in publishing and directing several New York galleries culminating with Daniel Newburg. He's had one-man shows in NYC, Houston, Minneapolis and Santa Barbara. His work can be seen at www.robyngeddes.net.

Give YourSelf Permission to Leave Your Family Business

by

G. Brian Benson

*"You owe it to all of us to get on
with what you're good at."*

—W.H. Auden

Six years ago I was running my family business. I had been
running this business, which was a successful golf center,
for 11 years. We had a driving range, a 9-hole golf course and
a retail golf store in Salem, Oregon called Cottonwood Lakes.
But I was unhappy; really unhappy.

I know a lot of people would give their "left arm" to have
that job, but I didn't feel like I was being my true authentic
self and that bothered me. Up to that point in my life I had
accomplished some really nice things. I rode my bicycle
across the United States, finished over 50 triathlons (including
four Ironman races), had a wonderful son and was running a
profitable business; so a part of me felt like I had a good
understanding of success and what that meant and felt like.
But I wasn't feeling that way at my job or in my life anymore.
I felt like I had this giant gift inside of me that wanted to come
out, but I didn't know what it was; I just knew that it needed

to be released. So, with a confused heart, I left the golf center and my family's business. I had no idea what I was going to do with my life after leaving ... but I trusted my decision.

Now, getting to the place of actually leaving the business was much harder than I just made it out to be. This was a job that had permeated through my being ever since I was a 7th grader driving a little tractor with a make shift wire cage on it to pick up the golf balls. I would effortlessly drive around lost in thought on warm summer evenings smelling fresh cut grass listening to the "thwack" of club hitting ball, compulsively picking up every single one of them come the end of the night so the customers could do it all over again the next day. I had grown up with that job, it taught me responsibility and gave me purpose. It provided me a consistent workplace throughout high school and during college while home on summer break. It also made me "cool" and gave me instant credibility amongst my peers, not to mention a handy place to take a date. But most importantly I had grown up playing golf, it was a sport that provided many happy memories for me as a child and a vital tool that helped my father and I bond; and that made it one of the reasons why it was hard for me to tell him I didn't want to do it anymore as an adult.

In my heart, I think I always knew that I wasn't going to be working at the golf center for the rest of my life. I felt an intuitive tug pulling at me early on during my 11 year tenure. It was the same tug that I bravely followed into triathlon racing after college ... but this tug wasn't quite strong enough or, more likely, I didn't have the courage to listen to it at that time to actually leave. But now it pulsed stronger than ever and wouldn't allow me to stay complacent in something that wasn't my true calling. That didn't make the initial conversation about wanting to leave the business with my father any easier. At first, I felt that I was letting him down. My thinking was that he had provided me with this great opportunity to run and co-own a business that most guys would happily say yes too. And I knew that he had secretly hoped that I would make it my own someday.

When I finally did gather the courage to have the chat, the conversation went much better than I could have ever imagined. I think much of the anxiety stemmed from my own fears of letting him down. He told me that he sensed I wasn't enjoying it as much as I had been at the start of my 11 year run and that he certainly didn't want me to do anything that my heart wasn't into or be someone that I wasn't. He also told me that he just wanted me to be happy. I felt very fortunate that my father understood my feelings and was able to let some of his own fears be tabled. After all, his oldest son just told him that he wanted to leave the family business, which he had planned to gift him, with no job prospects on the horizon for said son.

He also shared something with me that totally caught me off guard. He told me that if he could have done it all over he would have become a golf club professional instead of an independent insurance agent because he loved to teach and help others with their golf game (he had a very long and successful career as an independent insurance agent while we operated the golf center on the side). He sensed that he understood my need to find my true calling, whatever it may be, while I still had time to explore and find myself. All of the guilt I was carrying in regards to my departure was placed firmly there by myself and my own expectations of having this great opportunity presented to me by my father that I no longer wanted to be gifted.

I think many of us have been taught by our loved ones (as they were taught as well), that happiness and fulfillment come from fitting into a certain societal mold. The familiar model is to head to college, get a job, get married and have kids. Unfortunately, that expectation sometimes clashes with information we are receiving from our heart and intuition. At least, that was the case for me. As a result, I was initially caught in a situation of feeling like I was letting my dad down by following my heart. I am truly blessed that my father was on board with my change of plans. I was going to do it either way, but having someone you truly look up to and want to please give his consent made it much easier for me and allowed me to make the break cleaner than it would have been if he had disagreed.

Looking back on my experience at the golf center, with six years of perspective under my belt, I have no regrets. I learned a great deal about myself, people in general and business. I wouldn't change a thing. It also provided me with a stable income with which I was able to help support my son who lived apart from me in a different state and with whom I would soon be reconnecting with. But most importantly, it helped shape me into who I am today. It gave me the tools and knowledge, both tangibly and emotionally, that I carry forward. I am very proud of the fact that I followed my heart and listened to my intuition; and consider myself lucky that I had the courage to walk away from a secure yet unauthentic situation of running my family business.

When I stepped away six years ago I didn't really know who I was or what my future held. But what I did know was that I sure wanted to find out. I had to step away from something that I didn't love in hopes of finding something that I did. I feel like I am living an authentic life now. I have found happiness and fulfillment in writing, acting, and producing conscious media. I am accomplishing things that I never would have thought or dreamed possible. It wasn't until I left my job that I really began to see how alive I could feel, simply by being myself and following my heart. I am so glad that I gave myself permission to leave my family business.

G. Brian Benson is a creator and producer of conscious media. Writer, filmmaker, actor, TEDx speaker, award-winning author, poet, children's author, radio personality, finisher of 50 triathlons (including 4 Ironman races), cross-country bicyclist and someone that wants to help others be their true authentic self. He lives in Los Angeles. Learn more at www.gbrianbenson.com.

Give YourSelf Permission to Write Your Stories

by
Lynn Lipinski

I had been writing other people's words for so long that I lost confidence in my own voice. News releases, brochures, video scripts and speeches flowed from my fingers to my keyboard like water, while my fiction writing only trickled out like molasses.

My writing for corporations and organizations paid the bills, and I know I'm lucky to make a living doing any kind of writing. But my dream, one that goes back to my earliest memories, was to tell my own stories. Later, this dream morphed into a desire to write a "Very Successful Novel." I set the bar so high for this first novel that what I really did was set myself up to fail. Looking back, it is no surprise that this unrealistic goal sapped my confidence, and ultimately my motivation.

I worked on writing and polishing that first novel for so long that I think my friends doubted I would ever finish. I took classes, read books, participated in critique groups and hired editors. As the years passed and the storyline and characters evolved, I managed to get it out to a few agents and publishers despite lacking confidence in it.

What I really wanted was one of these industry professionals to exclaim how amazing it was and agree to publish it on the spot. Then they could tell the world it was good and sell a million copies. That was the only scenario I considered to be a success.

Someone else had to tell me it was great, because I didn't believe in myself enough.

But no third-party endorser stepped up. Though some of the agents and editors had nice things to say about my writing, no one wanted to represent me or buy it. Little by little, I allowed their criticisms to be part of my mental baggage, while I completely discounted their positive comments. This agent said my novel wasn't commercial enough so I must rewrite it. This other one said she didn't fall in love with my protagonist, so I should change how he acts. I gave them all too much control over how I felt about my own writing. I realized this attitude had to change.

First, I reflected on my values, a useful exercise I learned from the book *Give YourSelf Permission to Live Your Life*. I realized that I was giving too much weight to other people's opinions about my writing. I didn't value my own opinion of my work as much as I valued these strangers' reactions to it. That meant that I was basing my happiness, well-being and very existence on other people's behavior. And that was a losing proposition. Writing fiction to please others and garner commercial success had me floundering and frustrated.

I needed to flush the goal of publishing success and get back to the basics. What I really valued was creativity. Focusing on that, I mentally divorced the concept of creativity from publishing success. The two didn't have to be tied together in my mind. I could go back to the joy I'd felt as a little girl, writing stories and plays about leprechauns and faeries. I could write for the sheer pleasure of the art form.

I started out small by entering a flash fiction contest for stories just four paragraphs long. I didn't win, but that was okay, because I learned that I liked writing these little niblets of stories.

I wrote another flash fiction piece, and published it to my blog. Then I wrote another, and another. The fact that it was flash fiction made it seem bite-sized and manageable, not like the ponderous task of writing a 300-page novel. And I started to have fun writing again.

There are so many gatekeepers to fulfillment in the world. In publishing, gatekeepers are at every level of the game, and in general, they find it much easier to say no than yes. That's fine. That is their job and I cannot change that. But I didn't need to do their job for them by being a gatekeeper to my own fulfillment. That was something I could change. I had to believe that it was okay for me to put my writing out there — without the third-party endorsements I had been craving — for the simple reason that I wanted to. The Internet has made us all publishers if we want to be. I could publish my stories in my way on my own blog, for my own enjoyment and maybe that of a few readers.

Since I started publishing my flash fiction, I'm happier and more creative than ever before. Ideas and stories flow out of me like water instead of molasses. A second novel emerged from the corners of my brain and found its way to completion. My renewed zest for storytelling even helped me be more creative and prolific in my non-fiction and corporate writing.

I think my desire to write fiction was suffocated by the idea of having to produce a novel of some commercial or literary merit. When I gave myself permission to channel that desire into the pleasures of just telling stories to entertain people, I took a big step closer to my own personal fulfillment.

Lynn Lipinski is a writer and editor who pens non-fiction for a living and mystery fiction for fun. Through her firm Majestic Content Los Angeles, she creates print and online content for C-Suite executives, consumers, and everyone in between. She's the author of two books, Bloodlines *(2015) and* God of the Internet *(2016). Originally from Tulsa, OK, she now lives in Burbank, CA.*

Give YourSelf Permission to be a Small Kid with a Big Dream

by
Scott Mann

When I was 14 years old, I was hanging out with my buddies in Harrell's Soda Shop in the little town of Mt. Ida, Arkansas, where I grew up. This guy walked in through the front door and no one moved.

He had on a polyester uniform that looked like cardboard — not a wrinkle in it. He wore these massive leather jump boots with big, bulbous toes so shiny I could see myself in them. On his head was a funny looking soft, green hat that was unlike anything I'd ever seen before. It was a beret. As I watched him stride into the soda shop, I found myself pointing and saying, "That's me … that's me right there."

Laughter.

I was horrified to hear all the boys around me cracking up as I realized I'd just said that out loud. You see, instead of looking like John Wayne, or John Rambo, I looked more like Johnny Apple Seed. It must have been pretty comical for those boys to hear this scrawny kid proclaiming his goal to be like the warrior that had just walked in.

But, for the first time in my life, I didn't care. In fact, I didn't really hear their laughter at all. When I saw that soldier walk in I figured out, it doesn't matter how big you are — what matters is how big you dream.

So, I went right up to him and tugged on the bottom of his coat. "Excuse me sir — who are you? What do you do?" As he turned to look at me, his eyes softened from their predatory focus to take in the skinny little dude that was peering up at him. He smiled and told me he was U.S. Army Special Forces, a Green Beret. His specialty was getting in behind enemy lines and helping oppressed people stand up against tyrants.

I was hooked.

I spent the next 10 years of my life training and preparing to become a Green Beret. I failed every step of the way, but just kept going. One chilly October day in Fort Bragg, North Carolina, I earned my own Green Beret.

For the next 18 years of my Army career, I deployed to rough places like Ecuador, Colombia, Peru, Iraq, and Afghanistan. It came at a cost. I said goodbye to my wife and three sons no less than 17 times in 10 years. I lost 23 friends in combat and training accidents. But, here is the crazy part: I would do it all over again! I wouldn't change a thing.

You see, in those moments of chaos and conflict, I learned how to lead strong when trust is weak. I learned the importance of leaving deep tracks in this world by serving a purpose higher than myself, and how to "get surrounded on purpose" and meet people where they are, not where I want them to be.

Just three years ago, I retired from the Army after a 23 year career. As I looked out on the crowd of friends and family attending my ceremony, my gaze settled upon my three teenage boys. They had grown so tall and strong as they sat there looking at me.

It was hard to hold the emotion back as I looked into their eyes. I couldn't help but reflect back on the dream that had started when I was a scrawny 14 year old kid in Harrell's soda shop — not much older than they were.

In that moment, I shared with them something that had carried me through many rough miles and tough fights; something that had given me light in even the darkest places; a simple truth that kept me alive when hope was lost.

Don't ever give up on your dreams.

They are sacred. Dreams are the secret sauce to living into who we were born to be. For me, my dream of becoming a Green Beret was all I had. But, it was enough to carry me into a life that was even better than I ever dreamed it would be.

D. Scott Mann, LTC (Ret.), spent 23 years in the U.S. Army, 18 of those as a Green Beret. He teaches corporate leaders and their teams relationship-building techniques and is also the author of Game Changers *(Tribal Analysis Publishing, 2015.) Scott appears frequently on CNN, Bloomberg, Fox and Friends and dozens of syndicated radio shows. Learn more at www.mannup.com.*

Give YourSelf Permission to Have Financial Freedom

by

Trish Dolasinski, Ed.D.

A s a baby boomer growing up in the mid-'50s and '60s, my own parents were older than most of my friends' parents. Mom and Dad lived the experience of the Great Depression and always worried there wouldn't be enough money to survive. Therefore, I learned that money was earned and saved for a rainy day, and only spent on the core necessities of life. Those basics included food, shelter, and fabric (for my mother to sew our clothes). Mom was the queen of frugality, artfully managing the budget while staying at home to care for our family.

My father had a solid, white-collar position in the personnel department of a large firm. We were even among the first on our block to have a TV. As kids, my brother and I were not deprived, but I longed for a chance to have one store bought piece of clothing.

Keeping up with neighbors was never a problem because everyone had basically the same financial status as we did. In addition, with TV being a new medium, there were few ads to tempt us to buy more, bigger, better.

The societal utopia that protected me from the pressure of

wanting more came to an end during the summer I turned 14 and I got my first after-school job as a clerk in a five-and-ten-cent store. It was a time of great awakening, as I earned my own money and was free to spend it. When that first paycheck was handed to me, I bought a Peter Pan-collared gold blouse from a nearby clothing store. I pined after the fashionable item for days as I passed the display window. Although I feared telling my mother about the purchase, knowing she'd likely make me return it (along with a savings lecture), I was elated with my newly discovered freedom. To my surprise and great relief, my mother didn't object.

The experience was pivotal, as it gave me a sense of greater independence than I had ever known. I had actually done something that I never saw either of my parents do — buy something wanted, but not needed. This subtle rebellion in my early teens offered me a freedom from the family norms surrounding money. I was empowered and I liked it.

With college on the horizon and my father at retirement age, however, the tightening of the purse strings of my younger years bore down with herculean force. College was expensive and my Dad was no longer employed. The familiar anxiety of not having enough money and the pressure to "sacrifice and save" reared its unpleasant presence with a vengeance that was all too familiar.

To help with college expenses, my mother went back to work. But it wasn't enough. In order to remain in school, I had to take part-time jobs, sometimes two jobs, while carrying a full academic load. The model of hard work, stamina, and determination that underpinned my upbringing took over and I fell into step with what I knew. This time, it meant the difference between earning my degree — or not.

Although resentful that I had to work so hard when my friends did not, I learned another valuable life lesson. If I was willing to work, I could have what I wanted. The options were limitless and very enticing, including sorority membership, parties, more clothes, and even a summer in Europe with other students.

I met my husband of over 40 years now, during that two-month European adventure. He was a gentleman and a businessman who spent money on me. He also knew how to save, to invest, to create a budget, and to plan ahead for that rainy day. All I ever experienced about saving money meant sacrifice and pain. Now as a young adult, with his guidance, I began to see the value of saving as well as spending. A seed of the newly discovered freedom, and reconciliation with the painful emotions of saving, was planted in the soil of gaining knowledge.

With books as a longtime companion, I began to read about saving money. Suze Orman, author and financial guru, was someone with whom I could relate. Her books were informative and did not require an MBA to understand. My knowledge and confidence continued to grow as I encountered Karin Housley, author of *Chicks Laying Nest Eggs*. The key players in Housley's guide on how to invest in the stock market were not Wall Street financiers, but regular women, with kids, jobs, mortgages, and car payments, just as I. With growing confidence and *Chicks* on my nightstand, I launched an investment club with nine of my own girlfriends. Following Housley's step-by-step guide, we organized, developed by-laws, and met monthly to invest our dollars. The books were fun, I was learning a new language — how to save money by investing it.

Although our femme financiers group disbanded just before the economic plummet of 2008, the club was a major collective learning experience and our members profited from our investment decisions. I continue to invest independently to this day. I soon realized that, beyond my initiation into the world of investing, my day-to-day spending also needed attention. This was especially important as my husband and I were approaching retirement. Together, we developed and still use a family budget created in an Excel spreadsheet. With this common goal, we work together to track our spending, assuring that we save first, build in fixed expenses, and live within the bottom line — our monthly income. This has helped a great deal, especially when a true emergency has arisen and we were able to cover the expenditure from savings. Further, it goes without saying that we make sure our monthly credit card balance is always paid before the extras are considered.

From my growth and personal experience, I know that monetary values can be changed and it is never too late to do so. It doesn't matter what one's income may be, committing to regular savings and eliminating debt, especially that accrued from credit cards, is doable on any budget.

In addition, the key to true happiness is to build a sense of security through facing the challenge of creating financial freedom, becoming informed, and taking action to achieve the goal. Ignoring this important confrontation will only bring greater distress.

After six decades of life, I know that the security I enjoy today is not wrapped around the tangibles I could comfortably purchase. I was able to embrace my own financial freedom by saving, planning, and generally understanding that well-managed money can lead to a stress-free and guilt-free existence. A life of plenty and of peace, where I no longer struggle with the angst that once plagued me in my early years.

Trish Dolasinski, Ed.D. is a freelance writer and editor, as well as a talented group facilitator. She is also an adjunct professor at Grand Canyon University. Trish resides in Scottsdale, Arizona with her husband, Frank. They have seven gorgeous (of course!) grandchildren under age eight. They enjoy worldwide cultures and travel. Learn more at www.trishdolasinskiwrites.com.

Give YourSelf Permission to Make a Hard Decision

by

Heidi Kingstone

M y career as a journalist and writer began with two things: *serendipity* and *dogged determination*. The third element came into play many years later — *calculated risk*. Life affords you opportunities, but you have to act to make things happen, and, as I learned, you also have to know when to say "no."

That first brush with serendipity came when I went to see the editor of a magazine in Toronto, where I lived, about doing something completely different. In fact, at the start of my career, I had no idea what I wanted to do. In desperation, I thought my calling might be modelling, an odd choice for a number of reasons, not least because I loathe having my picture taken and always have done. Luckily, my conversation with the editor never got that far as she had other ideas before I had even broached mine. She asked me to write an article about fashion.

I suppose my DNA must have a mixture of the "yes" gene with a heavy dose of adventure woven through. Or, as I like to say, more guts than brains. I went home and somehow did the piece and realised from the first word I scrawled that I had found my vocation. Since that moment I have never looked back. The path has been strewn with hurdles, boulders, blowouts and the occasional tumble down the abyss and moving to London counted as the first obstacle, a town that hardly needed more writers.

During my first week, I had taken a tour bus to get a sense of the City of London and I still remember the thrill of riding down Fleet Street, historically the centre of Britain's print industry. I never imagined that I would work there. Ever.

I hadn't been in the country long when my then-boyfriend introduced me to a friend of a friend, who in turn introduced me to someone who worked at the *Daily Mail*, one of the UK's most popular national newspapers. Within a couple of months, I had started doing shifts in *Femail*, the department that concentrated on women's issues and topical features, and stayed for two years.

I always loved foreign news and when I took up my next post at another national newspaper called *Today*, as the late afternoon rolled around and I had filed my copy, I would sit at my desk, legs crossed yoga-style, reading the foreign pages waiting for the proofs to come back before the end of the day. This was, inevitably, the time the editor would amble down to the features department and magically appear in front of my desk.

Years later, after the aforementioned editor and I married and divorced, and I was in the difficult process of rebuilding my professional life, it dawned on me that I could pursue my dream of being a foreign correspondent.

I had started to write a weekly column for the *Saturday Star* in Johannesburg and moaned to fellow reporters over lunch that I had no ideas. One of the group suggested I do something on Saddam Hussein. In the mid-nineties, no one had any interest in Iraq, but I thought, "Oh well, why not?"

A day or two later, coincidentally, I received an invite from the Foreign Press Association to hear members of the Iraqi Opposition speak. At the end of the briefing, I went to talk to one of the two men, who I subsequently interviewed, and from then got drawn into the murky world of Iraqi politics. In 1998, nothing seemed less likely than an invasion of Iraq. Yet, in early 2003, I found myself in south-east Turkey trying to cross the border into northern Iraq with the rest of the international press corps in the run-up to what was the anticipated war, which took place a few weeks later.

The journey had been immensely stressful from the moment I began to plan it a few weeks earlier from London. But I finally got there, along with dozens of others.

We all massed on the border town of Siloppi waiting to traverse from Turkey to Iraq through a crossing that had been closed for years — the final tranche of the journey. All of us were headed to the big Opposition conference in northern Iraq.

While we waited in smoke-filled rooms, the topic of debate was about over-staying our time in Iraq. Many journalists planned to head to Baghdad so they could be in position when the invasion began, but this would mean breaking the agreement to return to Turkey after the conference. The discussion simmered in my consciousness.

It was a complicated decision for various reasons. While journalists from large organizations had huge teams behind them providing research, arranging tickets, transport, war insurance, drivers, fixers, translators and hotels, I just had commissions from great publications, but ones with microscopically small budgets.

As a freelance reporter, the company had no responsibility for my safety. Every decision I made was down to me. If the war started when I was there, for example, I would have no one to bail me out. At that time, the cost of war insurance for a single reporter was prohibitive. On top of that, the threat of chemical warfare loomed large and major media outlets supplied their staff with chemical suits. Those who commissioned me were not in the same league financially and thus unable to provide the necessary equipment. I had no experience and felt as if I was working in a vacuum, feeling my way through a dark, unfamiliar universe with no idea of what I was doing.

Throughout the days I was in northern Iraq, I debated the idea of heading to Baghdad or going to Kirkuk and waiting for the arrival of missiles and bombs. What kind of journalist would I be if I left? What would I think of myself, what would my colleagues think, and how would I ever really truly believe I was a good enough reporter? If I left, would I spend the rest of my life regretting this amazing opportunity? Would I be that journalist who had to say, "It could have been me." Would it have been akin to journalists in World War II who were there to see the liberation, and devastation, of the concentration camps?

That decision was going to have to be made as my time was running out. When I wasn't working, interviewing people, tracking down officials, or going to briefings, I spent much time talking to the then foreign editor of *The Economist* trying to decide what I should do. A good friend, he had bags of experience, a huge brain and understood the political situation as well as anyone. The threats of war were serious and imminent and the date of the advance unclear. If I got trapped in Iraq, no one would rescue me. If something happened, I would literally have to depend on the kindness of strangers. If the authorities decided to close the border again, and there were threats of that, we might all have to exit via Syria or Iran — countries we didn't have visas for, and that was true for Iraq. There were serious consequences to every single move.

In the end, Peter David, the foreign editor, said, "If your number's up, it's up." That was true but I wanted something more concrete, a guide, a firm answer. I didn't put my belief in fate. I never think of myself as fearless, and I certainly feared being killed or kidnapped or wounded or detained. Yet pulling me was this extraordinary opportunity. For years I had written about Iraq, I knew these people, this was my story, this was the chance of a lifetime for me and I didn't want to blow it because I was either too stupid or unprofessional, but I also knew, no story was worth dying for. Especially, not one like this that was going to be so heavily covered.

I was drowning. My Iraqi friend, who had lured me into the world of Iraqi politics, screamed at me to head back to London. He had close links to the Pentagon and was unequivocal in his advice. "Leave. Don't stay. Are you crazy?" Some of my new colleagues pushed me to follow them, saying everything would be fine. But, even I knew there were no guarantees. No one could predict what was going to transpire in the upcoming weeks.

Despite a lifetime and career of always saying "yes" for fear of saying "no," for fear of missing out (the notorious FOMO!), for fear of not pushing myself hard enough, I had to trust myself and my judgement. I had to follow my instincts and not listen to the prodding journalist who dared me to stay, merely to see what I would do.

That decision was to leave.

Sometimes I look back and honestly think I don't know how I did it. Ignorance and determination helped, as did sheer bloody-mindedness. I had no idea whether the decisions I was making were right or wrong and, even though I asked advice of more senior colleagues back in London who I trusted, in the end I had to decide for myself.

But, I did end up returning to Iraq on three more occasions

over the next twelve months, each trip equally trying and complicated and difficult, each beset with its own monumental hurdles, each time the stories were fantastic and those trips are some of the most memorable of my professional life.

I don't excel at giving myself credit for anything I do, but I have to acknowledge at some level that I made the right decision to go in the first place. Iraq afforded me the experience and confidence to go to Afghanistan and tread on very volatile soil, which I did in 2007. I know I made the right decision not to stay in Iraq in 2003, and that proved that I could trust my instincts, which are honed with experience. I learned that I take calculated risks, not enormous gambles, for better or worse, and that my judgement is often, not always, sound.

Heidi Kingstone, a native of Canada, is a foreign correspondent who has covered human rights issues, conflict and politics. Dispatches from the Kabul Café (Advance Editions, 2014), about the extraordinary life of soldiers, journalists, aid workers and fortune hunters in Afghanistan, is her first book. Learn more at www.heidikingstone.com.

Give YourSelf Permission
to Leave a Good Job
by
Ray Burkhalter

It was a beautiful sunny day as we drove past the golf course. My co-workers and I were on lunch break from our engineering jobs at a major automotive company and getting out of the noisy factory for an hour was nice. As the others discussed which favorite local lunch spot was the choice of the day, the golfers held my attention for that brief moment and it was then that a set of questions crossed my mind that changed the course of my life.

It was one of those seemingly simple chain of thoughts that ends up making you really step back and take a look at how your life is going. I, like many others, was in the midst of a career that followed my college education and I was working a good job with a great company. Ten years into this career I was doing the sensible, logical thing that everyone expected of me but I sensed a lurking feeling that the career path ahead of me didn't offer the kind of lifestyle I wanted. That future outlook included high stress, devotion to job over family and income potential limited not by my performance but by other factors out of my control.

That was a description of my future until that day on the drive to lunch when these questions crossed my mind: "How are those people free to enjoy this beautiful day on the golf course when the rest of us have to work? What are they doing differently than me? Can I do the same?" It was that train of thought that had my mind wide open to new possibilities when a friend handed me a copy of a book called *Rich Dad, Poor Dad* by Robert T. Kiyosaki. As I read it I learned of a financial concept I had never heard before: passive income. I began to realize that, based solely on my employee job, it would take decades to build significant passive income streams that would keep sending money to my bank account every month whether or not I went to a job. Being an entrepreneur had never been a serious consideration before but I realized that building my own business offered a much faster path to passive income and running a small business could allow me the flexible schedule to play golf on a sunny afternoon if I chose to.

But the pressure to stay in my current career was high. What would people think if I left a solid engineering career and struck out on my own? What if I failed and had to "fall back" on my degree and return to factory life? In the midst of those kinds of thoughts I realized that, if I was going to carve a new path, I would need to allow myself to experience failure and keep moving forward. No one else could make that decision for me so it was completely up to me to give myself permission.

I find that phrase, *Give Yourself Permission,* so very empowering. It reminds me that I have freedom of choice and the ability to create the future I want by making decisions based on my future plans instead of reacting to my surroundings. For me, the permission I had to give was to believe in myself, believe in those supporting me and to step forward in faith that things would work out. Doing so resulted in the creation of a successful real estate investing business that grew to a point that I was able to leave the engineering job without taking a pay cut.

So, how do you start a business when you are working a

professional job? For me the path included lots of study, training and connecting with those who were already running a business like the one I wanted. I had the help of my wonderful wife but still had to work after hours, on weekends and even give up my precious vacation time to attend educational workshops. However, the real game changer was hiring a business coach to mentor me along the way. With the wisdom of my coach helping me step by step along the way my wife and I formed a company and made the entrepreneurial dream a reality. I had a plan, built a team of professional experts and I was clear on the compelling reason for stepping into this venture because I knew that big challenges would come that would make me want to turn back. It was hard work building that business and there were plenty of days filled with doubts including the day I faced my biggest fear and gave my employer my resignation. The lump in my throat when I told my boss I needed to talk with him was huge, but I had a clear vision of the future I wanted, and that vision was stronger than the fear.

Giving myself permission to step away from that good job and follow my entrepreneurial dream was an excellent decision. There were challenges, yes, but also major benefits. One of the reasons I had a strong vision of the future I wanted was because of my dad's health. In 2006 I learned that he was battling dementia, likely caused by Alzheimer's disease, so the outlook was a progressive decline. I lived four hours away and fervently wanted to move near him and my mom to support them but the dependence on my engineering job didn't allow for that move. By 2010 he had also suffered a stroke and my desire to move increased and, by this time, I had taken enough steps down the entrepreneurial path to have new options. We were able to shift the focus of the real estate business to rental properties allowing us the ability to manage it from a distance and move back to my hometown. Doing so allowed me to spend the last two years of my dad's life with him, to be there to help with his care and to be there for my mom. That was extremely gratifying and it would not have been possible if I had not given myself permission to leave that "good" job.

Many people feel this same urge to follow their dreams but they end up submitting their permission to others. Sometimes the advice of others is helpful but it can also hold you back. When choosing to follow a dream it's wise to make the decision carefully, because it's a big one. But, if the feeling of certainty is strong enough then taking the step to give ourselves permission, despite what others say, can be the difference between living a life of regret and living the kind of exciting life that we choose to create. For me, giving myself permission not only gave me the ability to move near my family but also the freedom to work from home, create my own schedule and run a six figure home-based business. It has also allowed me to expand in ways I never thought possible only a few years earlier. Now I've given myself a new permission to explore skills I was not aware of in the area of teaching and training. The future is exciting.

Giving myself permission to leave a good job and follow my entrepreneurial dream was one of the best business decisions I have ever made and the positive impacts continue to ripple through all areas of my life. I am very thankful for the opportunity to share my story and I hope that in some way it encourages others to use their power of choice to give themselves permission to design the future they want.

Ray Burkhalter, a Tuscaloosa, AL native, is a business trainer and coach for emerging Solopreneurs. His work is devoted to helping Solopreneurs establish the business practices necessary to run their company successfully. His training program, Foundations of a 6 Figure Solo Business, was created specifically for that purpose. Visit www.solobizfoundations.com for more information.

Give YourSelf Permission to Dress for Success

by
Catherine Cassidy

"Catherine is a ray of sunshine, but she is painfully shy."
—My kindergarten report card

When I was 10, we moved to Chicago from Detroit. In Detroit, I went to a Catholic school (with a uniform) and had grown up with my friends. Chicago didn't just mean a new school where I was going to have to navigate making new friends; it was also a public school, which added a layer of *what do I wear* to trying to fit in.

I remember carefully picking out my outfit for the first day of school: my favorite striped and polka-dot leggings with an oversized t-shirt tied at the side. *Were they going to like me?*

At first, being the new girl made me inherently cool and mysterious. But that quickly wore off. Suddenly, I found myself without any friends.

My worried mother had me start seeing a psychologist. From this, I learned to realize that the "cool" girls weren't always the nicest. Learning to value kindness over "cool" helped me to make friends.

Even back then, when I wore my favorite clothes, it bolstered my confidence.

My own personal style and preferences have been pretty ingrained from a young age. My mom stopped shopping for my clothes without me at around 5 years old; I was always able to take part in my clothing decisions. So, in this new school with a need for a number of new clothes, my mother brilliantly gave me a budget for each season and I could buy what I wanted to build my wardrobe.

With this bit of style armor, I continued to show up and step out in school. I joined the Pop Warner cheerleading squad and I made new friends.

When it came time to look at college, I ended up choosing a school where I was the only one from my high school graduating class to attend as a first semester freshman. I took it as an opportunity to step into my confidence and move through my shyness.

While going through Sorority Rush and putting myself out there to make new friends, I found myself caught up in the desire to be "cool" once again … and it scared me.

Being in social situations where I knew no one, save for a couple of familiar faces, I was constantly outside of my comfort zone.

This first year of college, my style became even more important to me.

You would have *never* seen me wearing those Juicy sweats that were quite the trend at the time — at least not to class.

My college style may have been about tees, jeans and flip flops, but there was a lot of consideration for exactly which tees, jeans and flip flops I bought! I still had that clothing allowance and I discovered the beauty of designer denim. The frustration of trying to find pants that fit my bum *and* my waist just right finally came to an end!

Using my style as a tool throughout my college years and into my first years in the corporate workforce helped me to continue to build my confidence as I put myself in situations that were *not* within my ideal comfort zone. Still, my style was my armor.

When I graduated from college, I went into corporate fashion. My first job was in accounting — a foot in the door. When I was leaving for my next job, a colleague who I didn't work directly with commented, "Wait, I thought you already *were* a buyer?" I had dressed for the job I wanted ... and got it.

I *loved* my work as a merchandiser, getting to analyze sales trends, play with clothes and figure out what women wanted and needed for their wardrobe and self-expression.

Unfortunately, it wasn't exactly a collaborative environment.

All of my insecurities around being "cool" came back up. When my boss told me that I had to dress a certain way to get a promotion, I was flabbergasted. I knew I always dressed appropriately, so this was about *my personal style*. I received this feedback as still not being "cool" enough.

I was never going to be the visionary fashionista she wanted me to be. That just wasn't me. Give me classic, give me feminine, give me color and give me a little bit of fun.

This was just one of many things that told me I had to use my talents in a different way. I didn't resonate with the idea that you have to look or be a certain way to be "cool," which is what much of the Fashion Industry propagates. I *love* how the right pieces can make you feel beautiful, powerful, accomplished, and *confident*. That wasn't what we were selling there.

It was time to move on.

Close to the end of my tenure as a merchandiser, I gave the design presentation to buying. I wore my power dress and favorite heels. It gave me the confidence to *own* the presentation. As nervous as I was giving that presentation, all I received were compliments … on the work and on the dress. Something shifted in me.

I realized it wasn't the power of the dress, but what power the dress *allowed me to access*.

It took me 30 years to own my presence and my power. Now when I receive compliments on my style, I know it's as much about how I'm showing up as what I'm wearing. And my style was the catalyst.

When I was younger, I was afraid of my power. It made me a target. It made me get hurt. It made me lose friendships.

All of this made me dim my light. To try to not stand out to avoid being *hurt*.

Now, I recognize that by giving myself permission to own my power, presence and style, I give permission to the women around me to do the same. As we all do.

Our style is an extension of who we are. We are powerful, perfect and beautiful. Let's use our style as an outward expression of our inner selves. Let's also take advantage of this opportunity to communicate who we really are before we even say a word.

What is it that we are here to say? No point holding back out of fear. Let's take those first steps into our style power and own our own confidence.

I gave myself permission to show up, and I hope to do the same for you. Stand out and spread your message in *your* style power.

With over 12 years of experience in the fashion industry between Nordstrom, Robinsons May and BCBG, an undergraduate business degree from USC, and the launch of Ustyled, Catherine Cassidy has a unique blend of expertise in business, fashion, entrepreneurship and speaking. Ustyled supports busy professional women to evolve their leadership style and outsource their shopping. Learn more at www.ustyled.com.

Give YourSelf Permission
to Listen to Nature

By
Leslie Thompson

Pulling open the door to the herb shoppe was like stepping back into old world Europe. One was greeted by the co-mingled fragrance from the walls lined with jars of aromatic herbs, spices, teas and coffees gathered from all corners of the world. Bundles of colorful dried flowers hung from wooden beams, baskets of naturally fragrant exotic potpourri could transport you to India, the Hoosier forest, the Spice Islands or a rose garden. Melodies of the masters added to the ambiance that made the quaint alley-wide shop a haven for those weary of the hectic life just beyond that entry door.

My passion was herbs, gardening and designing with color, flavor and aroma. I had been offering my fragrant and culinary herbal creations at county fairs and mail order for eight years when a friend convinced me to partner and open a shop. The shoppe supported itself from the first day generating media attention that lead to adult education classes at the local university on growing and using herbs. I thought becoming a proprietor of this shop was a dream come true. In my naiveté, I thought moving the business out of my home would allow me to separate work from family and a partner would ease my workload. The partner quit after a year. It took effort to keep the shoppe from growing beyond my vision and capability. After three years, the dream had become a monster that isolated me from my family and invaded nearly every corner of my mind and moment of my life. Those demands robbed me of precious moments with my kids and exploring new aspects of my passions. The stress of employees, payroll, taxes, paperwork, creating products and writing a newsletter on top of house and family became overwhelming. My only personal respite was my daily five mile walk.

Up with the dew, the songbirds and the sun, my walk was a time of solitude, contemplation and regeneration with each rhythmic pace. Every day there was a gift, be it a scent on the breeze, beauty in a blossom, an amusing cloud formation or animal antic. One particular day I was asking the Universe, or whoever could listen to my thoughts, what I was going to do, why my dream had become a nightmare, and how had it all gotten so out of control? I was mentally and physically weary.

As I passed the woods a small mockingbird with a big voice attracted my attention with his endless variety of joyful tunes. A thought occurred to me: that happy little bird does not struggle in his choices. At least it appears he has no fears about tomorrow, about where his food is coming from — he lives in the moment and trusts his needs will be met. His life appears uncomplicated and simple. I then noticed the oak. It does not even move but stands strong in knowing the secret of success. Trees are some of the longest living things on earth. Granted they are not human with human responsibilities and worries but it provoked the thought that life does not need to be so complicated. It is our own "self" that complicates life in the endeavor to master control. At that point I made a choice to look at reality, quit living in reaction and move to something more balanced. I did not want my shoppe any longer! Herbs, gardening, healing through nature was my passion but retail was not. It was my ex-partners dream … I just got pulled into it. It was also a dream of my artist father who had passed away a few months before the shop reality came into view. Had I done it to fulfill my dad's dream in his honor? Although it was in my area of passion a shop was not really my dream; my family was my true love and I was missing out. No wonder I was not happy.

In that moment I voiced into the country air and beyond … I was ready to quit swimming upstream. I was suffocating — too busy to fill my soul's needs, too busy to do the little things and missing out on some of the big ones with my family. New knowledge and personal growth is as necessary to me as air, and I wanted my real priorities returned to their rightful place.

Later that very same week, a distraught woman walked into the shoppe with tears in her eyes looking to find some comfort in the cozy herbal atmosphere. She had just tried to buy a flower shop, the deal had fallen through and she was devastated. I off-handedly asked her if she'd be interested in an herb shop and within a month a deal was sealed and a check was in my hand. I was free to readjust my priorities.

Because of the simple joyful tunes of a mockingbird I began walking a new path of discovery. I now firmly believe in keeping things simple, letting life know my truest desires then getting out of the way, having faith that, if it is best for all, it will happen in its own way and time. Life is not miraculously perfect but, for the most part, gone is the struggle, the fear of failure, the fear of success, relying on others' opinions and most other mental garbage. When stress creeps close, I smile at the secret knowledge of joy in the birdsong or strength of the mighty oak and try to make sure I am not the one adding complications to life.

Now, living is gazing out of my home office window at a

pastoral view of cows chewing cud and ambling to the next tasty bit of grass, relishing the warm sun on their back and the breeze on their face ... then having that moment interrupted by the chaos of rowdy dirt-smudged faces running through the door with the latest creek find, such as the crawdad they dump on the desk, and listening to their adventures and the exuberant sound of their laughter ... priorities are back in order.

Leslie Thompson is nationally board certified in therapeutic massage/bodywork and professionally trained in clinical aromatherapy. She has written Notes from a Wingman: The Patient Guide to Wellbeing during Cancer Treatment *and is currently writing* Notes on Wellbeing through Aroma. *Leslie is evolving her vocation to include nature via the arts of language, fragrance, canvas and stone. Learn more about Leslie's projects at www.wingman.care.*

Give YourSelf Permission to Be Present

by
Vincent Avila

Like many people, over the years and throughout a successful career I became a very busy person. Naturally, the more professional responsibilities I took on the busier I became, juggling many things simultaneously which regularly bled into my personal life. Over time, I found myself spending much of my day focused on work related issues of the previous day or issues that would arise tomorrow. While it was often necessary to be extremely work-focused, I eventually came to realize that something was missing; something that I used to have that somehow escaped me.

Somewhere along the line I stopped the practice of being focused during the important moments of my life. I stopped appreciating the present moment the way I once had, and most often traded it away for some random, unimportant thought-wandering excursion about work, money or anything else other than the present moment. It's said that there is a time for everything. Instead of appreciating important times with family or friends, I found my mind wandering to work related issues. My cell phone and email became my new mental habit. I can only imagine how many wonderful moments I may have missed out on all because I wasn't really paying attention during that ladder-climbing period of my life.

I was in grade school the first time I heard a teacher offer the advice that we all should take the time to "stop and smell the roses," and though I was very young, I got it. It seemed obvious that we should take time to appreciate the good things that life has to offer. Of course, the focus of my roses back at that age was geared more towards ice cream cones and upcoming holidays. Fortunately, good advice is good advice and can apply at any age. Some things stick and the idea of stopping to take in a particularly special moment in life instinctively made sense and eventually found its way into the forefront of my mental behavior.

When I was 18 years old I was a soldier in the U.S. Army and living in West Berlin, Germany during the so-called Cold War; it was 1976. It was there that I recall making my first conscious effort as an adult to really take in a memorable moment; something that, for one reason or another, I wanted engrained in my memory. The incident occurred during a routine workday while patrolling the East-West border of the Berlin Wall (back when there was such a thing).

There was nothing spectacular about the moment itself, but I remember stopping at a border crossing and watching as a small group of men ran up and began taking photographs of me on my jeep, juxtaposed onto a couple of Russian and East German soldiers who were posted yards away on the other side of the border at Check Point Charlie. I recall thinking how fortunate I was to be here at that moment and appreciating the historical context of that time. I felt for the first time in my young life that I was a part of the "larger world," a feeling that I had not experienced before. For anyone else there it was likely just another day at work, but for me the moment was significant; something resonated deep inside, something about it felt special.

Acting on the advice of my grade school teacher, I made an effort right then and there to take in as many aspects of that particular moment that I could. The spring weather, the sound of the radio coming from the East German guard shack, and the smell of exhaust coming from the lead patrol jeep ahead of me are among the many details that made up that particular instant in time. I couldn't be specific as to why that scene and that moment felt important, but it did. Before leaving and moving on to the next checkpoint and without really knowing why, I told myself that I didn't want to forget anything about it — and I never did.

At the age of twenty-two, I became drawn to law enforcement. I found this line of work suited me and after a short time realized that I would make a career of it. It was during this time that I honed what I've come to believe to be the fine art of remembering, and the knowledge that I could only truly remember something that I was fully *present* for in the first place.

Looking back to my training days I recall being a bit amused to learn that it was now my "job" to account for all the details of significant events that occurred throughout the work shift. It meant that for every contact I made that resulted in an arrest or some other reportable incident I was required to write out what I saw, smelled, and heard and in many cases what my state of mind may have been. True, this was not an exercise in cementing memorial moments of my life, but it did help me establish the habit of noticing my world in real time as it was occurring. It helped sharpen my awareness of any given moment.

As time passed and my career progressed, I began having less and less appreciation for specific special moments in my life, both professional and personal. I found that I was focused more on some larger picture, frequently that focus was work related. Nothing wrong with that I suppose, but too often it came at the expense of moments that should have had my undivided attention, a potential "memorable moment." It may have been a dinner conversation with my wife, a homework talk with my daughters or maybe just some time looking out over the ocean. In any event, it likely was allowed to slip away due to my inattention.

My concern is not that I don't have the particular experience to reflect on today or sometime in the future, but simply that I missed the experience in the first place. Just because I was there doesn't mean I was *really there*. I can't help but feel that I've swindled myself somehow during that time.

Thankfully through a series of events and an uninvited health issue, I was given the opportunity to stop and assess my life. I say that I was *given* the opportunity knowing full well that I could have changed things on my own at any time, but didn't. Some people need a little kick before getting their attention and in this case I guess I was one of those people.

Regardless of how it came to be, I had a chance to remember what I used to enjoy and what made my life fun and interesting. I thought of several things, many of which I'm doing today, but it's the practice of being present during those moments that I deemed to be worthy of a memory that I most treasure. I think that it's because when I'm doing this I know that I'm not just being present in the moment, but actually living through what I've decided to be a special and memorable moment in my life; it's real, I can see it, I can hear it and most of all I can feel it.

Okay, so it's not like my life is one spectacular event after another — it's not. In fact, it's probably very similar to most everyone else's life. It's just that today I try to make it my practice to actively be on the lookout for a memorable moment. Though I don't always come across one, I always expect to, and that requires me to be present in the moments that make up my life.

I often wonder why that instant in Berlin was important to me; was it the idea of good over evil or a sense of duty or adventure? I also wonder how significant that moment, and others like it, might have been in the forming of my values later in life. My guess is that it was as influential as any other noteworthy experience I've had; isn't it our experiences, our moments, that have the greatest impact on the people we eventually become? If that is true, and I believe it is, then I owe it to myself and to the people I love to make every possible effort to be present in all the moments of my life. After all, I can never know when I'll come across one that is worthy of being one of my treasured memorable moments.

Vincent Avila is a retired police chief and the founder of Pace Setter Life and Career Coaching. He holds a bachelor's in vocational education (B.V.E.) and a master's in emergency services administration (EMER). He lives in San Diego, California with his lovely wife and dotes on his grandchildren. Please visit www.pslandc.com to learn more.

Give YourSelf Permission
to Find Your Golden Voice
by
Lynn Lipinski

People said he was cursed. Schoolchildren avoided him. His father sent him to live on the streets when he was a teenager.

Mali musician Salif Keita could have been a bitter, angry man, but instead he writes beautiful songs about life, love and fighting prejudice. His most recent is the plaintive "Folon." The word *folon* means *the past* in Keita's native tongue, Bambara. As the song goes, "In the past/ no one wanted to know/ In the past, whatever happened, you could not speak about it/."

Keita has lived through political turmoil, spending 15 years in exile during Mali's military dictatorship. "Folon" is about his homeland's return to democracy, but it could just as easily be about Keita's own life. Born albino, he was ostracized by his village and his family and left to live on the streets as a teenager. He found his voice and his salvation in music. Today, he has earned a place among the best and brightest on the world music scene and is frequently called the golden voice of Africa.

"Music is my life, my freedom. It gives me the opportunity

175

to talk to people. To tell them what I want and what I feel," he said in an interview with *PBS NewsHour* in 2015.

Cast away by his family, Keita made his own living in Mali's capital, Bamako, by drawing on his heritage, peppered with his own experiences as a pariah. Music and storytelling came naturally to Keita, who came from a family of griots, or storytellers, who have kept West African history alive for thousands of years through words and music. His big break came in the 1980's as leader of West African super-group Les Ambassadeurs who rode the global music wave with their fresh take on afro-pop.

Keita's albinism, a genetic condition that causes the skin, hair or eyes to have little or no color, also caused his blindness. But looking back on his life and his success, he demonstrates nearly boundless resiliency and optimism. "If I were black," he told *NewsHour* "then I wouldn't have had this opportunity to be popular in the world."

When he was young, Keita wanted to be a teacher. Today, as the father of several albino children, he splits his time between family, music and his eponymous global foundation for the fair treatment and social integration of people with albinism.

"Albinism is not a curse, but a disease which, like any other, needs to be treated with care and love," he told South Africa's City Press in 2014.

He sent a powerful message from his life in the song "La Difference": "Some of us are beautiful, Some are not/ Some are black/ Some are white/ All that difference was on purpose."

He found lightness and humor in his journey from outcast to one of the continent's most well-known musicians. "If I were black, I would have had good eyesight, and I could be a teacher for 40 people," he said. "But now, I'm a teacher for a million people. That's funny."

And as he sang in "Folon," "In the past, people did not want to know/ today, people want to know."

Lynn Lipinski is a writer and editor who pens non-fiction for a living and mystery fiction for fun. Through her firm Majestic Content Los Angeles, she creates print and online content for C-Suite executives, consumers, and everyone in between. She's the author of two books, Bloodlines *(2015) and* God of the Internet *(2016). Originally from Tulsa, OK, she now lives in Burbank, CA.*

TRAVEL & LIFESTYLE

Give YourSelf Permission to be Persistent

by
Geoffrey Kent

M y success in business stems from the permission I gave myself to be persistent. Above all, I followed my dreams wholeheartedly and believed in my vision.

Growing up on the family farm in Kenya's Aberdare Highlands was an idyllic childhood for a boy. I spent my days riding, shooting, camping in the bush and exploring untamed Africa.

I was a born entrepreneur, with the ubiquitous dose of maverick tendencies. I started my first business at age 15 selling elephant hair bracelets in Nairobi. It proved to be very lucrative, enough so that I was soon able to purchase my first motorcycle.

The only problem was that my school didn't allow them, one of the many rules that interfered with my notion of "living life in the fast lane."

A year later, I was asked to leave school even though I had excelled academically. The bike was the reason they gave for my expulsion. I returned home to live on the family farm. My father was not pleased, and our domestic life hummed along with deep tension. He wanted me to do something "serious" with my life; something in contrast to what he had done by immigrating to

Africa in the '30s. But I wanted something different. I wanted adventure.

A huge argument with my father sent me packing to explore Africa on a new motorcycle. At just 16-years-old, I told my parents I was leaving. I bought a tarpaulin and a sleeping bag from the Salvation Army in Nairobi, and built a frame for my two-stroke motorbike to hold petrol on one side and water on the other. I ventured bravely — perhaps naively — out on my own.

Carrying dried meat or biltong in my helmet (we never wore helmets in those days) and a map of the continent, I rode more than 3,000 miles from Nairobi to Cape Town — the first person to make the trip by motorcycle. As was often the case in parts of Africa, political and civil unrest made for frequently dangerous and uncertain passage. Looking back, I often wonder how I survived.

Once in Cape Town I managed to sell my story to a South African newspaper and get paid enough to sail home ... first-class to Mombasa. That experience made me realize I had a passion for travel.

Fearing what I might do as an encore, my father packed me off to the British Royal Military Academy Sandhurst. After my training, I was commissioned into the 5th Royal Inniskilling Dragoon Guards and saw service in such far-flung countries as Aden, Bahrain, Oman, Cyprus and Libya.

I was assigned as aide-de-camp to General John Frost, the hero of the Battle of Arnhem, whose story was retold in the film *A Bridge Too Far*. He insisted everything had to be done impeccably, sometimes under impossible circumstances.

When I was with the General on manoeuvres in the desert, he gave me orders that would later inform my vision for Abercrombie & Kent (A&K). "When I get to Kufra Oasis I don't want to be uncomfortable," General Frost had said. "We'll have the exercises and fire ranges during the day but at night I want what I usually have."

Wanting to ensure that General's dining experiences were as much like home as possible, I arranged for an engineer to make a refrigerated truck to keep everything cold. This became the inspiration for the business idea of combining adventurous travel with luxurious accommodations.

In 1962, five years after leaving Africa, I returned home to help set up Abercrombie & Kent with my parents. They had been forced off their farm in the run-up to Kenya's independence.

We had an idea for a travel company. My vision was as clear as a bell: adventures full of activity during the day, with total comfort at night. I knew instinctively this was what I wanted to do with my life. My mother was an early supporter and helped with logistics. My father oversaw the finances, but with much skepticism.

Back then, the competition for non-hunting safaris had been putting on the market what could only be described as fairly lackluster. Mostly offering only a couple dozen tiny rooms and zero in-suite dining. The last thing a visitor wanted to do after a flight from London or New York was to locate an African market and then navigate his or her way around looking for a nice bottle of wine or appetizing foods.

A&K's early safaris were modest affairs conducted with little more than my mother's silver ice bucket and a Land Rover. As we booked our first few clients, I thought more critically about what people really wanted from a once-in-a-lifetime safari vacation. My experience with the General reminded me how important the comforts of home were, even in the African bush.

This idea lit something so serious in me that I knew I could not share it with my father. I decided that, whilst my parents were on vacation trekking through the Khyber Pass (which connects Pakistan and Afghanistan), I was going to take a trip to the bank.

I withdrew five thousand pounds, which was most of our savings. I was going to bring A&K to the next level.

In an effort at finding a way to make the experience more comfortable for our guests, I called my old army buddy, Corporal Taylor. I enlisted his help in building a refrigeration system for a secondhand army Bedford truck. We worked day and night and when we finally finished, we toasted our success with Tusker beers chilled on ice made from a generator connected to the truck.

One of my visions had become a reality. Abercrombie & Kent was officially the first East African outfit to develop mobile refrigeration.

I ordered tents from Low & Bonar, a Scottish textiles company that makes the best-quality tents and traveled into the city on a shopping spree for beds and furniture; blankets and linens; pots and pans; china and silver; Royal Crown Derby teacups and, in a nod to my mother, cut glass decanters for the wine and more silver ice buckets.

I laid everything out and packed it into trunks that were custom-made into the back of the Bedford. Then, I lined the trunks with thick layers of sponge rubber to protect all the delicate items during transport. On the sides of the truck I attached containers for spare fuel, emergency supplies, and first-aid equipment; and finally, I made a checklist to ensure each item was present. (Imagine arriving at your camp 150 miles into the wilderness and realising you've forgotten the toilet paper.)

In very little time, my men and I were able to erect four tents, each of them 15-feet across with a 6-foot deep veranda. The floor of every tent was covered with a groundsheet to keep out bugs, and then covered again with a beautiful rug. The walls of the tents rose about 12-feet and sloped somewhat inward. The entire area felt spacious and bright, outfitted with electric lights, bedside lamps, and lovely sprung double beds high off the ground.

The lavatories were located outside, near the tents. They were essentially cleverly, but elegantly, disguised deep holes in the ground. We would never stay at the same site for more than three days, so the conditions were perfectly hygienic.

Inside the tent we placed lovely Plastolene tubs for women to take bubble baths in, and out back we had showers for the men. Inside the suite we laid out a bottle of Scotch on ice, chilled Martinis, crystal wine glasses, and sideboards displaying fresh vegetable crudités, smoked salmon, and chocolate cake.

I looked at my men, and we beheld the total luxury experience before us. The whole scene was completely ace. I vowed that this marriage of adventure and extravagance would be the stamp that Abercrombie & Kent's brand would come to be known by: the Off the Beaten Track Safari.

When my parents returned from their trip, my mother shared my confidence that the business would succeed. My father, on the other hand, was not at all pleased with my antics. He retreated into his office with great reluctance at being taken on this venture.

Our gamble on my dream paid off. Over the following two years, we saw profits increase dramatically as customers flocked to our unique model. Even my father eventually came to respect my persistence.

That's not to say we didn't have our challenges. Like other businesses, A&K was deeply affected by economic downturns, civil unrest, and 9/11. To keep growing the business after our initial success, we have had to be both nimble and aggressive, and willing to make changes along the way. Vision is powerful, but it is also important not to get stuck doing the same old things, the same way — over and over. There were days that I knew I had to just weather the storms and try to survive. I could fight the battle again the next day, but I had to survive the day first.

At the heart of it all, I know that my unrelenting insistence that there was a market for luxury travel adventures allowed us to build and grow our modest family business into the internationally renowned luxury travel powerhouse it is today.

Geoffrey Kent is the founder and CEO of Abercrombie & Kent, the world's premier luxury travel company. He lives between Monaco and London and his new book SAFARI: A Memoir of a Worldwide Travel Pioneer (Harper Collins, 2015) colorfully recounts his globe-trotting exploits. Learn more about Luxury Journeys at www.abercrombiekent.com.

Give YourSelf Permission to Say "Yes"

By

Priya Rana Kapoor

People ask me all the time how I get to do the all the fun things I do — I tell them I just say "Yes!" Which is what I did in 2011 and ended up in India and learned three very important lessons — which will forever guide me.

I have been lucky enough to grow up with family members who seek new experiences. This often means we have to go out on a limb and try something even when we don't know what the outcome will be. My grandmother left home at 16 to dance on cruise ships and was able to travel the world in the 1930's. You should hear all her stories. My mother moved from Los Angeles to London after college and created a very different life for herself, and you should hear her stories, too! Growing up I had very strong female role models. They did not let sleeping dogs lie, as they say. Instead, they saw opportunities to enrich their lives and they took them. My grandmother was, and my mother still is, exceptionally inquisitive and this is certainly what has shaped my life and what I want for it.

I love to learn and I like to have different and new experiences. This is not to say that I have not lived a life rooted in consistency and family values. I have a small family that was comprised of my mother, sister and grandparents growing up. We all loved and supported each other and we regularly ate meals together. But we have all travelled out on our own at varying times.

I started early. When friends would invite me to their homes abroad my mother was more than happy to let me go. You learn so much watching other people's lives and interactions ... even at 10 years old! So, all I have ever really known was to say "yes" when someone asked me to do something new and interesting. Often, though, I would not know what I was getting myself into and rarely did I experience what I thought I was going to.

My father was Indian and my mother is American. My father shared very little about his heritage and I knew virtually nothing about his side of the family. He died when I was 15. I had three half-brothers whom I did not really know. By the time I was in my late 30's we had reconnected through Facebook and we would all have a meal together once every 6 months or so, since we all lived in London. They would bring their families and we would catch up over Indian food.

At one of these dinners we were talking about India and I was lamenting the fact that I had never been there when my eldest brother turned to me, mid meal, and said, "I have an extra ticket for the inaugural Formula 1 race in Delhi, wanna come?" "Hmm, let's see?" I said facetiously. Then gave him a resounding "Yes!"

My other brother turned to me and said "It must be nice having your life, where you can just say 'yes' like that!" He went on to explain that it would be impossible with children and his commitments, and I get that. I don't have children and I also don't have a huge amount of money, but I choose to spend what I do have on experiences. Shawn Achor, in his book *The Happiness Advantage*, states that people who spend their money on experiences are happier than those who spend it on material goods.

So by late October, with visa in hand, I was off to India. It so happened I shared the plane with the entire Red Bull Racing team. I could tell this was going to be no ordinary trip, in more ways than one. I was also going to be there for Diwali, the Hindu Festival of Lights. It is a very important holiday and celebration much like Christmas. Have I already mentioned that I was super excited? I was beside myself, really.

The plane landed at Indira Gandhi International Airport in New Delhi at 6am. As I exited the terminal I was enveloped into another world. It was, after all, just the airport pick-up area, but the essence of the scene was strangely familiar. The sky is perpetually orange with pollution in Delhi and this makes for a rather ethereal tableau. The shadows stretched long from the dawn sun and airport business was as usual, but something stirred inside me. I knew this scene, and in that moment I thought to myself, "Now I know why I am the way I am." I felt like I belonged, like my DNA was linked to the soil and the energy of India. I had never been to India and had not been raised by any Indian traditions. In fact I was very Western, but all of a sudden I understood everything. I liken it to when adopted people say that while growing up they just felt something was missing but did not know what it was until they were told they were adopted. I never thought anything was missing growing up, but once I "found" a part of me in India, I knew something had been missing my whole life.

As I toured Delhi, this almost primal sense of belonging stayed with me. I am clearly not completely Indian and yet I garnered no attention at all as I walked down the streets on my own. At first, I thought I was doing a good job of blending in, but then it was almost as if I was invisible. Even when visiting the Taj Mahal not one child knocked on the window seeking pencils, treats or money. I would see them at all the other cars, but not ours. I cannot explain what was happening, but it took travelling to my ancestral home for me to become whole, even though I did not know that I had a piece missing. *I came to understand that every fibre of our body recognizes and reacts to its environment, so we better pay close attention to what we put it through.* However, this does not mean I was ready to move to India or embrace a whole new life.

My half-brother was my host for the 10 days I was there and he made sure to have many activities and parties planned. Most evenings we visited with friends at their homes or clubs in New Delhi. Diwali was celebrated with neighbours with candles, food, a puja and fireworks. Our host graciously allowed me to assist the priest with the prayers and ritual in the family shrine. I took this to be a great honour ... but talk about trial by fire. I had no idea what was going on; it was conducted in Hindi and I am sure I made a few faux pas. It was all so lovely and people could not have been more welcoming.

During the day I would hire a car and visit the sites, and each day I would be enveloped in the orange hue of polluted air that seems so comforting and safe to me for some reason. India really is magic, the people wear huge smiles and the colours are vibrant beyond imagination. There is enormous poverty and some "interesting" infrastructure. Some western companies have built moderate sky scrapers in the business districts but they sit on unpaved roads. Traffic is very heavy and routinely impeded by a cow in the middle of the street. Cows are sacred in Hindu culture and cannot be touched, not even to move them out of the way. So there is a delightful juxtaposition of cow, car, motor scooter and the occasional elephant on the public thoroughfares.

One evening, in a taxi on our way to another festivity, I asked my brother who we were visiting this time.

"We are going to see our cousin." he replied.

"Well, she is not really our cousin is she?" I asked, thinking that she must have been a fifth cousin 12 times removed.

"No, she is really our cousin, her father was our father's brother." I was stunned.

Not only did I not know I had a cousin but I had no idea I was ever going to meet such a close blood relative. She was also very welcoming. We performed a family ritual to honour the brothers of the family and we all had a lovely evening together.

I tried to find a family resemblance, and I really did try to feel a familial connection, but I didn't — and I felt bad. Whilst India had been so exciting and my brother had been so gracious and everyone had bent over backwards to entertain me, I was starting to get overwhelmed. Even though I felt a connection to the country, land and culture, I was starting to miss what I can only describe as my "people." I realized that those I grew up with, who nurtured me and were always there for me, where my true family. These were my mother, grandparents, sister, godparents, long-time friends of my mother's and my best friend's family. *I came to understand that blood is not always thicker than water.*

This experience has allowed me be much more present and loving towards the people I spend my everyday life with, and I no longer seem to long for something else.

For me, India was facinating and I recommend a visit if you are so inclined. I survived because I made sure not to drink the water and took very few risks. The traffic was horrendous, but I decided that there was nothing I could do about it. I also had to let go of my western hang up about time and punctuality. After all, I was in another country and I was going to sit back and let everything happen, whilst I observed with deep interest and recognition. I now live in California, but was living in London at the time of this trip. I have spent my whole life travelling between the States and the UK. I have lived in quite a few houses with a variety of people. I am often asked where "home" is for me ... and I never had a clear answer. After my trip to India, I have an answer. *My roots are wherever my feet are.* It does not matter where I live, all that matters is that I make where I am, at any given moment in time, a place where I am comfortable and am thriving. A location is just that, it matters whom I surround myself with and what kind of environment I build around me.

I learned these three lessons in India and I apply them to my life every day now. I love more whole-heartedly, I am present in my connections and I nest with more enthusiasm. All this because I said "yes" to a very kind offer to travel to a place seemingly unknown to me.

Priya Rana Kapoor, MMFT, is an executive life coach, author and motivational speaker. She is an avid sports watcher and traveler, with a dream of seeing Uluru someday soon. She aspires to own a closet full of cowboy boots and anything else with a bit of bling. Learn more at: www.priyaranakapoor.com.

Give YourSelf Permission
to Live Life's Great Adventure

by

Deri Llewellyn-Davies

I believe that life is a great adventure, and that we should live it with "no regrets" and leave this life totally fulfilled — to step up and live a life like that takes guts and hard work.

So the killer questions are: "Are you ready?" and "Can you handle it?"

Let's be honest, giving yourself permission to do something is not an easy thing to do. So many people say to me, "Yes, but I don't have discipline, or money or time" or some other excuse and I always respond the same way. The only things you're lacking are a burning desire and a massive purpose, then nothing can stop you!

I get it, I really do, we are all under pressure from different commitments in our life, whether they be work, family, financial constraints or the many other stressors of life. The things we would really love to do with our life go to the bottom of the list, and remain fantasies. For you to step up and prioritise your *dreams*, your *purpose* and your ultimate *why* need to be massive. Without those, your motivation will be a fad and won't last.

Don't panic, your dream doesn't have to be ground breaking,

world beating stuff. For most people it can be as simple as discovering art, exploring mindfulness or connecting back to your true health journey.

When I began my own great adventure, that I am now living fully, I was on the hamster wheel (you might call it the rat race or the corporate ladder). I think this will resonate with a lot of people. I was working hard in a career and, whilst it wasn't a big bad career and I wasn't miserable in my job, I had become trapped. I kind of liked what I did, there was no disillusion with what I was doing. I was good at business and was working up the ranks quite rapidly, but I was stuck on a one-track journey.

I was working ridiculous hours, commuting a long distance, working in the city and living to excess in my social life. I had always played rugby but had suffered an injury and had lost a lot of my fitness. I was overweight, my health had gone and my soul was on burnout — there was something massively missing, there was something I was yearning for, something profound.

To give yourself permission you have to start by going deep and looking inside to find out what the piece is that is missing for you. I think most of us are yearning for something, searching and pondering the inevitable questions: What are we here for? What am I here for? What is it all about? Ultimately, what is our purpose in life? Often it's not just one thing, it comes in multiple dimensions.

I had come to the point where I didn't recognise myself and didn't know who I was. Shortly after, I was hit by two blows; the end of my rugby career and the death of my father. I think a lot of us don't make the calls when we could or should, it takes something catastrophic in our lives to nudge us in the right direction. For me that was certainly the case, and the death of my father was ultimately what made me think and led me to giving myself permission to do what I wanted to do in life.

My father was a great man and a great influence in my life. Like many of us that have lost someone to cancer, it happened really fast. In the weeks that followed his death, what struck me the hardest was that my father had died with his dreams intact, never to be lived.

This sticks with me, and I think it will until the day I die. My father confided in me during the last days of his life that he had been a fool and that he had regretted not going out there and doing what he wanted in life. He always said he was going to do this, he was going to that, he was going to travel, he was going to do this with my mum — and he never did. It was always tomorrow, someday or whenever, but "someday" isn't on the calendar.

When your father admits he thinks that he has been a fool, had massive regrets and that he had died with his dreams intact, it makes you sit up, shut up and get s**t done. That was the point when I decided, "I'm going to live a life of great adventure with no regrets."

This meant that I had to be prepared to make tough decisions along the way because living a life with no regrets is not the easy path. My burning desire is to leave this earth feeling totally fulfilled, either aged 110 or during one of my epic adventures.

I started by exploring myself. "Know Thyself" was good enough for the Oracle at Delphi so I figured it was a good place to start. After much personal exploration and evolution with greats such as Tony Robbins, Dr. John Demartini and Mike Dooley, I realised something was missing. It was the visualisation of a future me, an older me, with my grandchildren sitting on my knee (at this point I didn't even have kids) and I realised I had nothing to say. Grandad did these big business deals and talking them through business acquisitions didn't really fit. That's when I saw my big why, my ultimate purpose — Adventure!

I always wanted to be an adventurer but figured that was for some other super breed of a person, not an average guy like me. This was BS and a crappy excuse. Suddenly I saw life for what it was, a great adventure, nothing less.

When I say adventure, I had decided at that point of my life "screw it," if I was going to go for adventure I was going to go big. I wanted to experience the best the world had to offer and really explore this wonderful world we live in. This led to my bucket list which I have dubbed "The Global Adventurers Grand Slam." This included the seven summits (the highest mountain on each of the seven continents), the two poles, the Marathon Des Sables (six marathons back to back across the Sahara carrying everything you need to survive on your back), the Jungle Marathon (six marathons across the Amazon jungle) and an Ironman thrown in to the mix! No one had done it before in that context, so I was going for a bit of a world first and that's where the journey began, it started with just a mere dream — as all things do! Then, I went to work ....

The thing you have to be prepared for when you give yourself permission is that not everyone will feel like you do about what you want to do and you might not get the support you imagined getting. Not everyone dear to me supported me. My mother, God bless her, who supported and was an inspiration throughout my childhood was anti-everything I did (and still is), because it's dangerous.

As I write this, I am very proud to say I have now completed the Marathon Des Sables, the Ironman and six of the world's highest mountains, culminating this year on Mt. Everest.

Everest was the ultimate challenge for me, the real test of commitment. It took 10,000 hours of work to co-lead the British expedition attempting a climb of the north face (the more difficult route) of what is already a brutal mountain. In April 2015, Everest was hit by the fiercest 8.1 earthquake in over a hundred years, all whilst I stood at 6300m (20,669 ft.)

on my way to advanced base camp! An experience that will stay with me for a lifetime.

We continued to Advance Base Camp just below the North Col, where I could get satellite communication. There we discovered the true extent of what we had just survived, as there were thousands dead on the other side of the mountain in Nepal.

Despite this we stayed.

Then the second earthquake hit.

We still stayed.

Three days and three nights below the North Col, and we were still prepared to go for a summit bid. I had turned back on other mountains but we had calculated the risk at this point on Everest and we still thought we had a chance. Eventually the Chinese authorities closed the mountain, forced us off and evacuated us. This saved my life as the third earthquake would have hit whilst we were on the summit ridge, and that would have been game over.

During the evacuation from the mountain I had time to reflect. I was fully ready and prepared to die for my dreams. I was playing full out ... and if I had died there and then ... I would have died with no regrets having lived life fully in all areas. That was a beautiful realisation. It took 10 years of facing my fears, making tough decisions, failing many times, but always getting back up as it's never over ....

Now I have to be true to that message, for my children, to help them to follow it. For me, not to do Everest and not to do my adventures wouldn't be being true to my message. So many of us sacrifice for our children, this is a very honourable thing to do and I get it, but I have seen so many people then regret and come out ten/twenty years later when the kids have grown up saying "I wish I had done that when I was younger" or "if I hadn't had you kids, I'd have done that." Well, the kids are watching. My daughter and I sat together, before I went away, my eldest was 7, and I asked her, "How do you feel about daddy going to Everest?" And she said she was sad and happy. I said, "Why are you sad?" And she said, "I'm going to miss you and I love you and I don't want anything to happen to you." I asked, "Why are you happy?" And she said, "Because you're the best daddy who does amazing things and you're going to climb Everest for me and I can go into school and tell everyone about it and show my daddy can do anything and so can I."

And so the adventures continue. A lot of people ask if I am disappointed, frustrated or bitter about Everest and not reaching the summit. The answer is "No." I'm blessed as I am still alive, and in living an adventurous life there is no failure, it's just the next adventure, and Everest isn't over ... I'll be back.

So my message is: give yourself permission to discover and step into your great adventure in life. Whatever it might be, find that missing part of you, your purpose, your big why. Ignite that burning desire deep inside of yourself and then go to work. Miracles come from action.

For me my father's death was the catalyst, but leaving a legacy for my children, to be inspired and motivated by, is what makes me continue. I want my children and grandchildren to think, feel and believe that they can do whatever they want in life, just like their daddy, and just like you.

Deri Llewellyn-Davies, a.k.a. The Strategy Man, is an international speaker, CEO, business strategist, and global adventurer. He is a father of three and lives in England, but is a proud Welshman. For more information please visit www.thestrategyman.com.

Give YourSelf Permission to Leap

by
Debbie Brosten, M.S.Ed

The spring of 1975 found me wondering where my life was headed. I had graduated with a bachelor's degree the previous spring, complete with a certificate to teach both elementary and special education. Problem was that 1974 produced a bumper crop of education majors and I didn't land one of the limited teaching positions. Plan B found me living back in my childhood home, working as a teacher's aide in a school for emotionally disturbed children. Even though the school was run by a prominent child psychologist and even though I was learning a lot from my on-the-job training, I wasn't content with my life.

To make matters worse, a girlfriend, Debbie Klein, was preparing for a trip to South America. One winter day as I moped across her bed while she sorted blue jeans and bikinis for her trip, my malaise was threatening to overtake her jubilant mood.

"I'm so jealous!" I told Klein. We were both named Debbie, but she was commonly referred to by her surname while I was often called Doll, my father's nickname for both my mother and myself. To differentiate us, one of my brother's friends had dubbed me Little Doll and my mom Big Doll.

"Ya know," Klein told me, "You have a teaching certificate. You can travel and get paid for it." At first I merely stared at her. She must have forgotten who she was talking to. I am not one of her more adventurous friends (or at least I wasn't at that time).

"Me, go overseas? I'm not sure I could do that." As my stomach heralded its irritation, Klein shrugged her shoulders.

"Well, you could write my friend Gail's sister. She's been teaching in Australia for the last year and loves it."

"I'll think about it," I replied, but I was pretty sure I was just appeasing her.

Later that night I thought about how sheltered my childhood had been. My three brothers, even the younger one, all took care of me. My mom helped me make most decisions. In high school I was quickly identified as Larry Brosten's little sister. He was two years ahead of me in school.

Unlike me he was part of the "cool" crowd. Friends clustered around him, every teacher knew him by name, even if he wasn't in their classes. It wasn't that I didn't have friends; it was just that my friends were a lot less notorious in high school. I was the dependable one, the one who did her homework, blended in, got good grades.

"You can travel and get paid for it." Klein's voice echoed in my brain as I lay in bed that night. Maybe it was time for me to take a giant leap out of my predictable life. What did I have to lose? The next day I obtained the address of her friend and wrote to her.

Not long afterwards I heard back. "Do it!" she said. "Life here is fantastic." She told me that the Australian government was recruiting teachers to teach in Australia for one to two years so their teachers could return to school to complete four-year degrees. A recruitment fair was being held in a college town not far away. Supplied with my resume, application and borrowed courage, I attended the event. More than a hundred teachers filled the crowded venue. I remember talking to someone who told me that only a dozen or so teachers would be hired from that crowd. Immediately, I decided I had no chance.

The interviewer for special education teachers was running late. It was the end of the day. She decided to run a group interview with five of us. I remember her stating an educational philosophy with which I did not agree. Figuring I was not getting the job anyway, I risked telling her what I had learned working with the child psychologist. I'm not sure if she was impressed with my ability to venture an alternative idea or if my background fit the profile she was trying to fill. Whatever the cause, I got the job. I would leave that summer for a year and a half in Queensland, Australia.

As my departure approached, I was filled with equal parts of excitement and fear. My father asked if I was sure I wanted to go so far away. I reviewed what I knew about Australia — kangaroos, the Great Barrier Reef and 17,000 homesick miles between it and the home I knew.

From the moment I arrived on Australian soil, I was amazed at how easy it was to make friends. The majority of teachers were just like me, new to teaching and alone. During a week-long orientation, we bonded over our shared situations. Friends were made, roommates selected as we got down to the business of exploring our new environment and getting ready to begin teaching.

We learned that baked beans on toast is an acceptable part of breakfast, gas is called petrol and sold in liters, and a student requesting a rubber (eraser) in class was typical.

One morning two weeks after school had begun, I walked

my normal route to the local train I rode to work each day. I had begun to recognize my neighbors and we shared morning greetings as they walked their children to school or set off for work. Whiffs of bacon escaped open windows. Purple jacaranda leaves swirled around me as I took in the sights which were so similar to a small American town, yet still so different. That morning as I stood on the train platform, schoolchildren in various colored uniforms raced around the station or stood quietly conversing in small groups. Clanging bells signaled the train's arrival. I entered a compartment with long cracked leather seats lining each side of the carriage. Citrusy shampoo smells mingled with someone's partly eaten vegemite sandwich as I leaned back in my seat. I was definitely not in Chicago anymore.

A smile graced my lips as I sat quietly amid a packed carful of children talking in lilting accents as they joyfully bantered back and forth. I was thrilled to be among them and surprised at how easy the transition away from my family and friends had been. Much as I missed them, I was not immobilized by their absence or their support. I realized that not only was I not remotely homesick, I was eagerly greeting each new day.

After 25-plus years of teaching on both American coasts, I retired from teaching two and a half years ago and moved to Bellingham, Washington, where I didn't know a soul. Since that time I've made friends, volunteered my time, and joined or started groups to support my interests. Just the other day I was talking to a woman in my prompt writing group. The subject of intimidation came up. When I mentioned a person who totally intimidated me, she squawked,

"You get intimidated?"

"If only you had known me before I went to Australia, you wouldn't be asking that question."

Her remark gave me the opportunity to reflect yet again how Australia had reformed my life. It taught me how connected people across the world are, no matter what language we speak or which god we petition. No longer was I the shy, fearful Little Doll who risked that epic journey, but instead a confident woman who embraced life with enthusiasm. Taking that giant leap to Australia changed the trajectory of my life. It taught me that what is waiting on the other side is always worthwhile, even if not always what I expected. Now I err on the side of leaping when faced with a crossroads in my life.

Debbie Brosten, M.S.Ed, relocated to Bellingham after retiring from a career in education. She delights in the serendipity of her travel-filled life and the people who populate it. Her work has been published in the Whatcom Writes Anthology *and* Memory into Memoir: A Red Wheelbarrow Writers Collection.

Give YourSelf Permission to Make Your Home Wherever Your Heart Is

by
Leslie Keeler Saglio

I remember moving 5,400 miles from Los Angeles to London, and leaving everything I ever knew for love — love for my French fiancé and love for the idea of adventure and possibility. We met each other online, a rather pioneer concept back then, but I've always been one to try new things and never stop exploring. I remember feeling so refreshed to have met someone so outside my circle and completely outside my culture. It opened not just my heart, but my eyes and life to a whole new world and experience. Sure, there were people that had their opinions on long distance relationships, but I kept the faith and knew that, if I wanted to have a serious relationship, it was time I took myself seriously and stopped caring about what other people thought. Nine months in, he proposed and of course I said "Yes!" We were ready to take the plunge and I was ready to move country.

I was leaving my "American dream" as a successful entrepreneur who owned a condo by the beach, drove a European convertible and was mother to two adorable yorkies. So many friends and family were in awe of my huge decision, finding it hard to believe I would leave such a good and comfortable life. For me it wasn't the end of a good life, but rather the start of something foreign that I could only imagine if I given the chance. And so, I gave myself permission to create a new life for myself and to make a new home wherever my heart would be.

Were those first years hard and did I miss all the comforts of my hometown? Yes. Would I go back and do it all over again? Absolutely. Living in a foreign country had its ups and downs, but giving myself that permission slip 10 years ago truly paid off. Through those challenging times outside my comfort zone, I started to see myself, and experience the world, so completely different — a life so beautiful, beyond anything I could have ever imagined.

The first year was difficult (especially that first London winter) as I would count down the days, and possibility, of moving back to Los Angeles. It wasn't until I had my first child and established my London roots that I finally surrendered to the experience of life as an expat. I began to reach out to other new and young mothers as a way to stay connected. I went to baby classes, new mom meet-ups, and pretty much anything I had time for. And soon, I realized there were other people who shared my same fears and dreams as an expat wife and mom. I found that, through the birth of my child, I too had been re-born. I finally started to fully embrace my situation. I not only survived but thrived in this new life abroad, opening my heart with love and gratitude, enjoying the present moment and allowing myself to "just be." I began to see and experience life through a different lens. Life was full of so much texture and I knew it would never be the same.

That first year, I found travelling to other countries also helped the process. It was time I took charge, and advantage, of my situation, just a few hours plane ride from so many different cultures and people. I travelled places I had only seen in movies and met people I had only read about in books. Travelling and experiencing other parts of the world helped to constantly put my life in perspective. I found that learning how to adapt while on holiday abroad helped me learn to appreciate my new London life back (in my "new") home.

I also learned just how important community means as an expat far away from family. Once I started making other American expat friends and celebrating American holidays, it was a great way to get grounded and feel centered thousands of miles away from everything I used to know. Tradition can absolutely be adapted, enjoyed and treasured just as much with dear friends abroad as with dear family back home. My expat friends soon became my family.

Last year, bearing witness to my father on hospice care, I made the same decision, rooted in love and not fear, to move country. I finally agreed with my husband to move to Barcelona for a change in lifestyle. For years I wouldn't even entertain the thought, as London had finally become home. So much so that when I went back to the States I sometimes felt like a tourist in my own hometown. But, once again I gave myself permission to create a new life for myself and to make a new home wherever my heart would be. And it's been an incredibly wonderful experience for all of us. It's been a time and place for us to re-connect to ourselves and to each other as a family, as we share and grow from each and every experience.

Expat life in a new country has been a completely different experience, not only because of the contrasting culture from England to Spain, but mostly because I'm a totally different person. Today, I'm not the same person compared to that 20-something who moved 10 years ago 5,400 miles across the pond. This time around I immediately cherish the differences and relish the challenges, embracing everything as an opportunity to grow and evolve, for both my children and for myself. I absolutely trust that, by giving myself permission to make home wherever my heart is, has made me a true citizen of the world. I'm able to live and work with so much love and compassion for others. It has also served me well as I'm now better equipped to support my clients and students as an international coach, yoga teacher, writer and speaker.

Everything and everywhere now is a new and beautiful experience — through both my children's and my own eyes. With an open heart and grander perspective, life has so much more to offer. Life is always changing and every moment can be an adventure and possibility of growth and evolution.

Where we live does not define us. We can never lose our identity. Home is not defined by the confined walls of your house or apartment building, but rather, home truly is where the heart is. From my experience of 10 years living abroad as an American expat in Europe, I've learned the heart can absolutely expand to include many other people and places. By giving myself permission, I now have, not just one home, but three — my heart is even more open to giving and receiving as I have friends and extended family all over the world!

Give yourself permission to change, to feel, to step out of your comfort zone, to grow, and to evolve. It's in those moments of change that we truly know what we're capable of and can begin to experience life more beautifully.

Ten years as an American expat, Leslie Keeler Saglio knows what it takes to overcome the challenges to create a new and happy life. As an international coach, yoga teacher, energy healer, writer and speaker she guides others to live a stress free and happy life. A Los Angeles native, she lives in Barcelona with her French husband and two young children. Learn more at www.LeslieSaglio.com.

Give YourSelf Permission
to Travel the World

by
Wendy Profit

Sometimes something very small happens that changes the course of your life in a very big way. I was in the last semester of my four-year university education and was about as unsure of my future as anyone could be. I was in default mode, about to earn my B.S. degree in Psychology for lack of any better ideas. I was contemplating a job or further education, and I figured a master's degree was a waste of time and money without a plan or a purpose. I never had any good answers to those questions: What do you want to do with your life? What are you going to be when you grow up? What do you want?

Cowgirl – Astronaut – Rock star unfortunately didn't work as well in pre-adulthood as it did on the playground.

One day, late into my final "lost" year in college, my favorite professor posed a better question. He asked, "What would be the biggest risk you could take in your life right now?" I thought about it for a second and the riskiest thing I could come up with was to drop all my "plans" for the future and travel around the world alone. I had taken a semester or two of Spanish in high school, and Italian in college, but I had no knowledge of foreign currency, how to get around on my own, and no experience traveling solo.

World travel was exotic and adventurous. It seemed out of my reach, impossible. It was the furthest thing my little imagination could grasp. In my small-town reality you went to school, got a job, got married, bought a house, had kids and lived happily ever after — if you were lucky.

My professor considered my answer for a moment and responded with something like, "You can buy a Euro-rail pass for a few hundred dollars. There are inexpensive youth hostels everywhere filled with a network of backpackers about your age. It's common for young people to travel after college. It's actually very easy." In that moment, everything changed for me.

Why had no one told me this? My college professor had just taken the biggest, wildest and most impossible dream I could conjure and placed it in the palm of my hand like a little acorn. Not only was it possible — it was, in fact, EASY! How could I not do this?

So I graduated from university with what I deemed a useless degree and a big dream. For once in my life I had vision, focus, purpose, and passion! It was interesting to share this dream with people. They responded either with enthusiasm and words of encouragement, or dark warnings and threats of doom. No one would ever hire someone so irresponsible. How dare you leave the path that society has carved out for you? You'll get behind. Bad things will happen. It's dangerous for a young woman out there alone. You're so brave! Go girl! — and all that ....

What I never imagined was the push-back I'd get from my own family. My mother had always been my biggest cheerleader. She learned early on that to tell me not to do something was the very impetus for me to do it. However, the woman who told me I could do anything, be anything, suddenly revealed her more conservative self. For her, traveling the world and living an exciting and adventurous life was secondary to securing a sound financial future. Perhaps a better dream for me, she suggested, would be to get a job at Disney World, (I could be Cinderella or Snow White!) marry an investment banker, or follow in her footsteps and become a wheeling-dealing real estate broker.

I finished school, found an entry-level job in my hometown and started saving money for my Big Adventure. Meanwhile, Mom enrolled the two of us in a house-flipping Real Estate Bus Tour Seminar. This was a course where you ride around in an air-conditioned tour bus exploring impoverished neighborhoods, looking at homes that can be purchased at affordable prices, remodeled cheaply, and flipped for a profit. There are now reality TV shows based on these teachings, and I must admit it ignited an interest in real estate investment that has benefited me to this day. But something far more important happened on that Real Estate Bus Tour Seminar ....

You see, Mom got sick and was unable to go on the bus tour, so I agreed to go without her (it was for my future, after all). The bus drove us around all morning while the instructor, through a megaphone, regaled us with the wisdom of linoleum and cheap bathroom fixtures. I learned all sorts of things:

- Don't turn it into your dream home, just make it look better.
- Use neutral colors throughout. It may be boring, but hot pink doesn't sell.
- Remodel it cheaply and sell it for a profit.
- Look for a good roof and a good foundation.
- Avoid plumbing and electrical issues, as these are big-ticket items.

We stopped for lunch at a local restaurant and I sat down with a fellow named Neal. He and I talked a little about real estate and then the conversation turned to travel. He told me about visiting an Indian reservation in Utah and his experience with the Native Americans. I told him about my dream to explore the world. We finished the tour, shook hands and exchanged numbers.

Six months later — on my birthday — I received a certified letter from Neal. It was a round-trip ticket to Europe that he'd purchased in my name with his frequent flier miles. I was floored, excited, confused, and suspicious. Was he trying to seduce me with this gift? What was his motivation or purpose for doing this? Could he possibly just want to give me the biggest, most important gift of my life? I sat there shocked and slack-jawed, turning the ticket over and over in my hands. Was it real? Yes! Was this really happening? Yes! Could I really take this ticket and fly away across the ocean to lands unseen? It came with a note that said, "No strings attached. It cost me $13.89 in taxes. I was inspired by your passion to travel and wanted to help make that happen."

He included his phone number and it was a good hour or so before I summoned the courage to make the call. I cautiously dialed his number, he answered. Timidly I said, "Neal? This is Wendy ..." He immediately reiterated what he had shared in his note and added, "I saw the excitement in you as you told me about your dream to travel and I just wanted to help. This is my way of helping and I hope you have a great adventure."

I learned to check out the post-card stands first. If you don't know where to go, the post-cards tell you the town's claim to fame. Also, asking other travelers where they've been and getting their recommendations on fun things to do is a really good way to find interesting and unusual places.

One of my favorite memories was riding a scooter around the island of Santorini in Greece. It's a mountainous island and I still remember the moment when the road rose to a height in which I could see the beautiful blue Mediterranean on my left … and on my right. I was in the middle of the Mediterranean Sea all on my own, wind in my hair, bugs bouncing off my teeth. It was July and my return flight home from London was scheduled for August. I giggled and basked in the freedom, knowing that there was no way I was going to make that flight.

Thank you Neal, and thank you Dr. Busby, wherever you both are. Your gifts gave me permission to live my life. Since then, my adventures have included most of Europe including Great Britain and the Greek Islands, the Caribbean, Egypt, an African safari, the Great Wall of China — with much more to come.

I love seeing the world go by from the window of a train, walking the long halls to the bar car and having a drink and chatting up strangers. I love arriving in a new town without a clue or a plan. It really is easy. I never feel as alive as I do when I'm on the road. Time is accelerated. I am able to live in the present fully. There is no time to dwell on the past or plan for the future, just unbridled living.

Wendy Profit is a singer/songwriter, blogger, and short story author. She was a featured artist in Girls Rock!: Fifty Years of Women Making Music. *When she's not performing in local dive bars she enjoys urban farming and renovating her 1903 Victorian home in South Central Los Angeles. You can visit her renovation blog at www.ourhousefrancis.blogspot.com.*

Give YourSelf Permission
to Open Your Heart to Service
by
Arlene Dreste

It took a near-fatal accident to alter the course of my life, to help me find my purpose and to give myself permission to open my heart.

It was a beautiful sunny day in August 1995. My boyfriend, Joe, and I were getting ready to go to a friend's funeral. Before we left, I had a premonition that something was going to happen that day that would change my life forever. It was nothing more than that, no details, just an uneasy feeling. I had no idea what lay ahead or just how deeply my life would change before that day said good-bye and entered into history. That was just the beginning though, this metamorphosis occurred over many years, and I am still changing and growing.

That evening, while Joe and I were at the gas station filling up the Harley, I noticed it. I saw the minivan that would be the tool of change. Why did it catch my eye? It was waiting at the light ... or was it waiting for us? It happened just as we left, I remember the impact of that van, its grill coming up on us and literally tearing us apart. Joe landed on one side of the street and I on the other, with the bike and the van between us. When they took me away in the ambulance, I looked over at Joe and thought I saw him moving. I thought he was all right, but he wasn't. That was the last time I ever saw him.

We had been together for 13 years and I never got to say good-bye. I was in the hospital for two weeks and so was unable to attend the funeral. Why had I survived that accident? Witnesses said they were shocked I had. There had to be a reason.

It was during my stay in the hospital that something happened that would, years later, be the key to a major turning point in my life. It came in the form of a magazine. A friend brought me my mail from home and in the stack was my copy of Earthwatch magazine. It is the publication for Earthwatch Institute, a non-profit organization that supports various, mainly environmental, scientific-based studies around the globe. In this edition was an article about a project that involved the radio collaring of mountain lions in Montana.

This definitely piqued my interest, as I had planned on becoming a wildlife biologist until those plans were interrupted by the untimely death of my parents when I was a teenager. I went to work as a veterinary assistant for small animals instead. I inhaled the article and thought about how I would love to get involved in something like that. Maybe this was my chance to make up for lost time. Then I looked over my broken body and my broken life and thought, "Yeah right, and just how is that gonna happen?" I allowed myself the liberty to daydream and make plans for an adventure when I got out. It had been a long time since I had been excited about anything, or dared to imagine that something good could happen to me.

After losing my parents, and especially my dad, I lost my enthusiasm for my childhood dreams. I spent my 20's, and the first half of my 30's, wild and angry. I was living, but far from alive.

While I write this piece though, I reflect on my life and realize that I have been living a life of service since I was very young. I just didn't think of it that way. I always liked helping and I was good at it. I did pet-sitting for neighbors. I helped my dad on the truck, and my mom with her job at the doctor's office. However, my life of service would temporarily be abandoned as I struggled through my everyday life.

I was a drug user for many years. Cocaine was my drug of choice and that made sense given its great anesthetic properties. All of the pain of grief and loss surrounding my parents — and then Joe — would vanish. I wanted to be numb, and so I was. However, I could sense myself itching to make changes. Life had to hold something more for me, but how would I find it? I had tried before to get clean, but it was only ever temporary. Then the accident happened, and I fell further into the abyss.

Those were some of the toughest days of my life. Why was I still here? Again, why did I survive that accident? I wasn't working and I had no home. My childhood home had been foreclosed on. I rented a van that became a home for me and my dog and cats. I was on the verge of giving up. I couldn't take it anymore. I felt I had no purpose.

I looked at my "fur babies," which included three kittens born the day Joe died. They needed me. Who would take care of them if I was gone? I wouldn't let them down. That was the beginning of the turnaround. I started thinking about going into rehab, but it was divine intervention that ended up having a hand in my new start.

In my friend's living room, God spoke to me and said, "You have to leave New York. Your life is not here anymore. Put your life in My hands and I will take you to where you're supposed to be." I did just that. I packed up my fur family and left that life behind. That trip was my rehab. I got clean on 8 November 1996 somewhere on the road between my past and my future — and I've stayed clean ever since. After all, I was heading to my destiny, to find my purpose … and this I wanted to feel.

In December, I arrived in my new home in Arizona. One month later I went to work for the local transportation company. Thus, my life of service resumed. I loved this job because I got to help people by taking them to doctor appointments, shopping, or just family visits. There were a lot of elderly people there and the "little old ladies" quickly adopted me. Sometimes, I even had to climb through windows when they forgot their key inside their house. Later, when some of them became frailer, I became their caregiver. I have worked with developmentally disabled young adults and, most recently, with Native American youth at an elementary school on a reservation. My life of service changed directions as a result of this last job as I now had more time off.

My first summer break from school was spent doing a road trip with my dog. I knew it would probably be our last together and we had a very special time visiting over 30 states and seven Canadian provinces. It was magical.

In December of that same year, the tsunami struck Southeast Asia. Watching that tragedy unfold made me realize just how much need there was in the world. Being grateful for that special summer I had just spent, and all my blessings, I decided it was time to give back. I decided I was going to spend the next summer vacation doing volunteer work. This was when I gave myself permission to reopen my heart to service.

I remembered the Earthwatch magazine I had read at the hospital. I knew I wanted to get involved with their wildlife projects. Before I could even call them to inquire, a card arrived in the mail asking if I'd like to receive their project catalogue! I hadn't received anything from them in 10 years.

There was no space to reply "hell yes," so I simply checked off, "yes, thank you." When the catalogue finally came, I remember dropping it on the table and it automatically fell open to the Lions of Tsavo project. This had been my dream since childhood, to be with the lions of Kenya. This idea had consumed me since seeing the movie *Born Free* when I was just three years old. I felt this was more "divine intervention" blessings for my decision to serve.

Being in Kenya for two weeks tracking lions was the most wonderful experience of my life. I got to help the researchers collect data for their study. This would be the first of four Earthwatch projects, as well as a project in Borneo with another organization working with orangutans. As a result of my most recent Earthwatch project, tracking chimpanzees in Uganda, I have returned to college to finish my degree as a veterinary technician.

When I am not traveling the globe, participating in one project or another, I am home, helping on a local level. Whether it's volunteering at the local pound, doing animal rescue on the reservation, helping kids, or taking care of my elderly friends, this is my life.

I made a promise to God while I was on the road after I left New York that if He got me out of that mess, I would help whomever, wherever, however. I do my best every day to keep that promise. I have found my purpose.

Arlene Dreste was born and raised in Queens, New York and currently lives in Arizona with her family of rescued dogs and cats. She's been a vegetarian since the age of sixteen, and her favorite songs are "Born Free" and "Here Comes the Sun." Her mission is to create a kinder, gentler, more loving world.

Give YourSelf Permission
to be Uncertain

by
Teresa E. Olson

I half leapt, half collapsed onto the train car entry steps. My 48 pound suitcase landed on the back of my legs then slid to one side. I clutched the handle so it wouldn't fall back onto the railway platform. The carriage doors closed behind me. Rome Termini train station; not my favorite place. The passengers heard my panting and looked my way. From the floor, sweat dripping off my nose, I asked "Perugia?" They nodded. At least I got on the right train. I'm doing this travel thing, but I'm not doing it well.

To be fair, I never expected to be chasing trains in Italy. Less than two short years ago I was content and settled. I had a husband, a home, two dogs and a cat; a beautiful garden, and a cabin in the mountains of Montana. I had a great job that I loved too, with all my heart. At 42, those were all the things I wanted in the world and I had invested 17 years pulling it all together. I was quite pleased with the identity of me. I looked good on paper and in conversation. So it was shocking when a tiny hairline fracture in that illusion of my life became the Grand Canyon, and I found myself divorced. I was left with just my car and a decent bank account. *What the hell just happened and where am I?* I immediately began preparing to re-invest and re-establish myself. Hurry up, gotta be me again, gotta rebuild me again.

In my nearly empty, rented apartment, I took a break one night from Realtor.com to read an inspirational blog. It happened to have an invitation to spend a month in Bali to "write your story." Not even knowing where Bali was, I completed the application. Favorite Writers? My Mom, Ann Frank, Aldo Leopold. Spiritual tendencies? Kindness, the Universe and the 12 steps. What's your project? A memoir, but deeper. An exploration of how I came to be in this place by transposing my journals and dissecting every entry. There must be keys, nuggets of information which expose where I went wrong. How can I avoid being in this place again? This broken, fractured, shattered place that wasn't part of my plan — and shouldn't have been part of my identity at all.

I was accepted to the workshop and the waiting began. Six months I waited, but I wasn't waiting for my trip. I was waiting to get back so I could buy a home, get new pets, plant a new garden and reinvest for my retirement. My life was on hold and in the interim, I felt like I didn't exist. How could I? I had nothing. Nothing to show who I was except the one single thread of my job; thank goodness for my job.

Bali finally came and I did write for an entire month. But I didn't write an investigative piece about how I could identify and blame myself for going in the wrong direction. Instead I spent every day writing a delicious novel about potato farmers and women who wanted to support their community by transforming their own lives. I wrote, and I hired a local motorcycle/cab driver to take me to a gym every day. For $3 I rode on the back of Nyoman's motorcycle through the bustling Ubud streets to the air conditioned gym. He waited there for me to finish. Afterward he always wanted to take me places and show me the beauty of Bali: a waterfall, rice farms, or the monkey forest. Sometimes I would go, and sometimes I had to write, but always our rides were filled with laughter and fun and somehow I felt a bit of myself there on the back of that motorcycle.

The day before I left Bali, Nyoman picked me up for our usual ride but took me instead to his family's temple. He spoke such broken English I didn't understand most of what he said. But as we walked around I could hear in his voice the story of his father coming to the temple, and his father's father, and so on. My heart ached for a family, identity and belonging, and that knowing of who you are because of where you are.

I had completed the first draft of my novel. But, what did that mean to me? Sure, I felt accomplished for completing something I'd never tried before. I had made many new friends from the retreat who I loved and adored, but I otherwise felt unchanged. I was ready and anxious to resume the rebuilding of me. I returned to my little Montana town and my great job and started house shopping again.

But something was shifting. Something undetectable and indescribable. The funding for my job with the State was up for vote in the current legislative session. I had known for a long time the vote was coming and I was confident the State would continue the important work my program offered. My one thread of identity was solid, I had no worries about it. Until I did start to worry.

I started to worry that my job funding *would* be renewed. I worried that I *would* buy a house and rebuild me. I actually wanted my job funding to get cut, so I would be forced to make a big change. I started confessing to my friends, "I kind of want to keep traveling; I kind of want to edit my book into a reasonable manuscript." I heard myself say these things, but couldn't make sense of it. How could I want a home and identity and uncertainty all at the same time? How can both those desires reside in one person?

But they did, and I came to realize I wasn't going to find peace by rebuilding me. I couldn't just replace what I had minus the husband. My foundation was gone. So be brave, I thought, become a new person — fearless and adventurous. I decided I would quit my job and write and travel. But for some reason, I felt physically sick about it, so I chickened out. Then, I felt sick about not doing it. Why is this so hard? Everyone posting on Facebook tells me how great it feels to be fulfilling my purpose. I tried again a month later and decided yes, I would quit my job and write and travel for a while. When the nausea returned, I chickened out a second time. Angry and frustrated with the constant indecision, I adopted a dog and put an offer in on a house. "You're going to settle down and shut up about it," I told myself.

Meanwhile, the legislative session approved the funding of my position, as I knew it would. Instead of great relief and calm, I felt even more angry and frustrated. Angry that the Universe didn't hand me forced change on a platter. Now I was going to have to decide: certainty, or uncertainty.

When the counter offer on the house came in, I took one step; I turned the offer down. When my friend battling an empty nest said she was desperate for a dog, I took one more step forward, and tearfully offered her mine. With fear gripping my pen, I gave written notice on my apartment. With more tears and sadness, I told my boss I was giving notice … my last step. I explained how I had loved every day of my nine years there, but I had an opportunity to try something new. An opportunity to not rebuild my life, but instead to find my home and maybe my self within.

It's been a few months now, I have been traveling and writing. I have visited Italy, the Midwest and all over

California. Before I return to a job and an address, I plan to see India and maybe Peru with more of the U.S. in between. I'm still not brave and adventurous; and I still don't travel well. I often feel sick to my stomach and cry easily when I see someone loving their dog or visiting friends and their families. Still, I am giving myself this gift. This precious and painful gift of time to be uncertain. In this uncomfortable and scary place I am rebuilding myself. Not with things or a beautiful home, but with the unfamiliar, and new, rich experiences. I find myself there, on the back of that motorcycle, in the smile of a stranger, in the sunset walk on the beach. Little bits of me, gathering them up, settling them into my heart, which has become my home.

Teresa E. Olsen plans to return to Montana at the end of her travels and resume work as a water conservation specialist. She's grateful to her friends who supported her through her adventures, and her Mom who inspired in her the creative outlet of writing. She loves cooking, camping, bird watching, and the Green Bay Packers.

Give YourSelf Permission
to Sail Away
by
Paul Bain

When Priya asked me to write an article for the first edition of *Give YourSelf Permission Magazine* I had just been promoted at work and was "too busy" to give an article my full attention at the time. To my shame, I simply emailed her a manuscript (still not quite finished) that documents the slightly surreal story of a crazy sailing voyage her close friend Kate and I undertook over 20 years ago in the first flush of our relationship. She rightly rejected it and asked if I would be able to put something together for a later edition. I hope this will do …

In 1993, frustrated by the cost of living, cold and stress of London life, we made the choice to go against the prevailing opinion, advice or wishes of our friends and family. With our first new baby still unbreached, we rented out our flat in London, found and bought a sailboat in Florida and took off through the Bahamas and across the Atlantic, sailing through the hurricane season and returning to the UK during the treacherous North Atlantic gales. Kate was 21 and I was barely 26 and the journey was life changing for us.

At the time, it was a huge step to take into the unknown. With next to no sailing experience and little understanding of what life would be like in the confined space on board, our decision was certainly questionable, but to undertake the journey with our first child still not walking or talking we were frankly considered to be quite mad. Our journey took us through some of the most beautiful but unforgiving islands in the Caribbean and home, while poverty and the dangers of tropical storms and gales tested our boat and relationship to straining point.

We experienced challenges ranging from dangerous infection to theft, from adverse meetings with sharks to being serenaded by whales, from drinking with mercenaries to dealing with frustratingly small-minded officials. We survived mechanical breakdowns and appendicitis, with a smattering of foul weather, sandy beaches and rum thrown in. We lived in a bubble, away from the sensationalism of TV and newspapers, our life almost a vacuum — sometimes frightening, sometimes blissful. It was a story of dreams, reality and hardship laced with danger and not a little laughter that added a core of strength and wisdom to our relationship that would be impossible to replicate, as well as a unique sense of individual confidence that has enabled us to explore life without worrying what others think. There is no "right way" to live this life. Ultimately, we as individuals have the choice to decide which way we will explore the infinitesimal time we have on this Earth — Kate and I, in the infancy of our relationship, chose to explore and embrace our own insecurities and those of human nature, and in doing so found out the true properties of love … I wonder, what is your choice?

I write this article on the eve of my 49th birthday and with the benefit of almost a quarter of a century of hindsight to draw on. Kate and I are on holiday, sitting in a bar overlooking a stunning beach in Cambodia, a few months away from our 25th wedding anniversary, and I can tell you categorically that neither of us has any regrets about that choice whatsoever. Since we sailed the Atlantic, we have explored a wealth of different cultures and countries, by train through Africa, on motorbikes through the jungle in Vietnam, and in a tiny rally car driving across a third of the globe from London to Outer Mongolia. We have chatted, argued and ultimately learned from a vast range of different people. But perhaps more importantly, we have balanced the frenetic wanderlust of our youth with a settled life in the UK, living in a lovely house in a beautiful city and working in "normal" jobs. Our eldest son Jack is now 23 and both he and his younger brother Olli love to travel and have the confidence to explore new cultures; their natural willingness to experience other worlds and cultures was certainly born from hearing tales from our own adventure and Jack in particular is longing to do something similarly crazy — the only difference between his choices now and the decision we made years ago is that we are happy to encourage him in his quest, with the confidence that life only really works when you embrace opportunity and reject your fear of the unknown.

I am no guru and I have made many mistakes along the way in life, but have no doubt that Mark Twain's advice is as valid today as when I first took it literally in 1993 — he was, perhaps, one of the first to expostulate the *Give YourSelf Permission* message:

"Twenty years from now you will be more disappointed by the things that you didn't do than by the ones you did do. So throw off the bowlines. Sail away from the safe harbour. Catch the trade winds in your sails. Explore. Dream. Discover."

—Mark Twain

Paul Bain is Director of Studies at Seaford College. His other adventures include rallying a tiny minivan 10,000 miles from London to Mongolia and forging the Vietnamese jungle on a motor scooter. Paul lives in Chichester, West Sussex with his family. His next challenge? "Central America's rain forest, of course!"

ACKNOWLEDGEMENTS

This was a most rewarding project work on…a true labor of love. I feel that, by now, I know and love each of our authors and can't wait to get to know them even more. For, without them, there would be no project, at all! The incredible bravery and dedication it takes to share your personal accounts of your life with the world is truly inspiring and, for that, we are humbly grateful.

Priya, James and I would also like to extend our heartfelt thanks to the many people that helped us to bring this project into reality. To Leanne, thank you for the brilliant idea of transforming the Give YourSelf Permission Magazine® into an anthology; what a wonderful vision! To Julie Colvin, we extend our gratitude to you for your dedication and hard work on the retreats that brought so many of us together.

We also want to thank Sarah Brandis for her tireless efforts in digital marketing to get the word out on social media about the Give YourSelf Permission® brand, introducing all of our authors and with the promotion of this book.

To our designers, along with Cathy Henszey, who designed the most beautiful magazine I have ever seen, we thank you from the bottom of our hearts. To Lynn Lipinski for her initial edits on the magazine and her steadfast support and friendship.

And, finally, to our families and friends who *are* family, we are humbled by and so appreciative of your unwavering love, support, encouragement and patience during this entire process, start to finish.

Thank you for believing in us.

Nanette Stein
Editor, *Give YourSelf Permission Anthology*

GIVE YOURSELF
PERMISSION™

HOW TO BE A PART OF THE GIVE YOURSELF PERMISSION TRIBE

Everyone has a story …
Share, Teach, Learn … with a dash of Inspiration!

How can I submit a story?

Many of us don't give ourselves credit for the amazing things we've accomplished in our lives. We often don't feel like we've done anything significant but, I bet you'd be surprised if you really looked at your life and the decisions you have made.

If you find that you *have* given yourself permission to do something around risk-taking, life changes, personal growth and successful outcomes, we would love to hear it!

This is your chance to share your story with the world (not to mention become a published author) and to help another fellow human being along their own journey to giving themselves permission to live their best life!

Simply visit *www.GYSPermission.com* and enter your details into the "Share Your Story" box. You will receive the submission guidelines and up-to-date information from us.

How can I send you feedback?

We thrive on feedback and you are now part of the movement. We will be publishing more anthologies so please visit *www.GYSPermission.com* for updates and we welcome your ideas and inspiration for specific topics that you might like to see more of. E-mail: info@gyspermission.com

How can I get more information about life coaching and the Give YourSelf Permission® Empowerment Programs?

Priya is available for 1-2-1 life coaching sessions. We will also be adding new Give YourSelf Permission® e-courses, workshops, webinars and live events on a regular basis. You can sign up to be on our mailing list and you will receive special offers. All that information can be found at gyspermission.com/coaching.

How can I follow you on social media?

Follow us on twitter: @GYSPermission
Like and follow us on Facebook: *Give YourSelf Permission to Live Your Life*
Come join the party on Instagram: *priya_gyspermission*

We look forward to meeting you!

OTHER PUBLICATIONS IN THE GIVE YOURSELF PERMISSION SERIES

Give YourSelf Permission to Live Your Life
(Balboa Press 2014) — Priya Rana Kapoor, MMFT

Give YourSelf Permission Magazine® — Fall 2015
(Permission Media, Inc.)

About the Creator

Priya Rana Kapoor, MMFT is an executive life coach, speaker, author and founder of the Give YourSelf Permission® Empowerment Program. She holds a master's in marriage and family therapy from the University of Southern California and a certificate in coaching from  Coach U. She grew up in London, England. Priya has been a guest on NBC's Today Show, BBC Radio Asia and Hay House Radio. She now lives with her husband in Santa Barbara, CA, but travels back to London as often as possible to see clients, friends and family. She has dreams of traveling to Australia, India and the Middle East for work and pleasure.

About the Editor

Nanette Stein started writing her first blog in 2011 as a hobby. After her family faced multiple tragedies, she turned those experiences into lessons to help both herself and others by writing about how she has coped and learned from these life-changing events. It's her dream to help others understand that they are not alone and that there is a way out of pain and despair. She took the leap in November 2015 and

© D'Arcy Benincosa

"retired" from her 18 year career as a Registered Radiographer to pursue a writing career, full time. She now has the immense honor of being the editor of the Give YourSelf Permission® Anthology, an actual dream come true.

CPSIA information can be obtained
at www.ICGtesting.com
Printed in the USA
FSOW02n1228070917
38302FS